THE PARENT

THE COACH

THE MENTOR

Empowering our youth, parents and coaches and bringing awareness to bad behavior that affects our student athletes on and off the field of play.

Anointed Press
PUBLISHERS

Cheltenham, MD
www.anointedpresspublishers.com

THE PARENT
THE COACH
THE MENTOR

Empowering our youth, parents and coaches and bringing awareness to bad behavior that affects our student athletes on and off the field of play.

by: Archie R. Beslow

The Parent. The Coach. The Mentor

©2014
Archie R. Beslow

ISBN 13 - 978-0-9860719-8-0

DISCLAIMER

Although the author and publisher have made every effort to ensure that the information in this book was correct at press time, the author and publisher does not assume and hereby disclaim any liability to any party for any loss, damage, or disruption caused by errors or omissions, whether such errors or omissions result from negligence, accident, or any other cause.

To purchase additional books:
www.archiebeslow.com
www.anointedpresspublishers.com
www.amazon.com

Also Available on KINDLE

Ingram Distribution

Cover Design
Anointed Press Graphics, Inc.

Published by:
Anointed Press Publishers
(a subsidiary of Anointed Press Graphics, Inc.)
11191 Crain Highway
Cheltenham, MD 20623
301-782-2285

FOREWORD

When I was 10 years old I played my first organized football. It was with Boys Club #2 in the District of Columbia. I was good enough to start at running back and safety. We won our first few games and were atop the league. And then we played Boys Club #5 which also was undefeated. It was an experience I will never forget as long as I live. The score was tied 0-0 late in the second half. A receiver took off and did a hook pattern right in front of me. He caught the pass and as I went to make the tackle, I did everything wrong. I dropped my head, dove in desperation to bring down the receiver and grasped nothing but air. He stepped around me and scored the only touchdown of the contest.

Without question, I had singlehandedly lost the game. I felt awful.! As I took that seemingly interminable walk back to the sidelines, thoughts raced through my head that I would never play again, my teammates would hate me and the only time I would touch another football ball would be while looking at one in a store. . I just knew it was the end of my fledgling football career. I dreaded facing Coach Wyatt. I was convinced he would yell at me, put me on the bench forever and move on to someone else he could better trust with that responsibility.

But, he did not yell. Instead, he patted my on the helmet and gently said, "We'll work it out." He seemed to know right away how devastated I was and how fragile my confidence was at that point. The next week at practice he worked on my technique, showed me some good pointers on tackling but, most of all, helped to rebuild my self-confidence.

He continued to play me. Later in the season, we faced the same team again. Tie game, 0-0. They had the ball and I was playing safety. The QB dropped back to pass but by then I had learned to read his eyes. He let the pass go right where he was looking. I stepped in front of the receiver, grabbed the interception and returned it for the game-winning touchdown.

When I read Coach Archie's book, The Parent, The Coach, The Mentor, I immediately reflected back on that experience.

My coach, Julius Wyatt, understood the game but, more importantly, he understood how to work with children. Those are the very qualities possessed by Coach Archie that he so eloquently captures in his book. He is the parent, the coach and the mentor—a man who understands and loves children, a man who, at once, is a mentor and a teacher.

His book is a primer, a how-to manual for emerging coaches, for those who simply want to help young people stay on a constructive path, and for parents who want to understand the best ways a caring adult can help their children grow and develop. It is a compelling, sensitive treatment of his relationship with and tutelage of children entrusted to his leadership by parents with high hopes and aspirations for their kids.

Coach Archie's book shows he is a phenomenal youth coach who comprehends the importance of education, character building, spirituality and fun. He teaches kids how to play the sport but most importantly how to play the game of life. It is no wonder that many of those he coached maintain contact with him long after they have moved on.

I would be comforted knowing that Coach Archie is coaching my child, and so should other parents.

Mayor Vincent C. Gray
Mayor of Washington, DC

FOREWORD

Sports are a powerful medium for building character in young people. Beyond the winning and losing, sports provide a context where young people can learn about themselves as well as about life in general. While most will not become professional athletes, the sports experience is invaluable in them developing life survival skills. Learning how to cooperate with others for a common goal is something young people gain from sports. Getting in shape and disciplining their bodies lays a great foundation for future endeavors. And what about respect for authority and following orders so that you can execute effectively in game situations as another example of the life skills gained from sports. These and many more benefits come from participation in sports.

No one is more important in this process than the coach. The coach is the most important component in the equation. The skill the coach displays can mean the difference between an enriching, meaningful experience or one in which the young person actually is set back by their participation. Between these two extremes coaches have various degrees of influence on their young players.

This book is about a man who has mastered the skill of coaching. Okay I will admit he is not on national television. He is not a professional coach of one of the top teams in any of the four major sports. But I am not exaggerating when I say he is one of the best there ever was. He is passionate about coaching being a means to an end. He is not just interested in his teams winning the championship so that it can reflect on his ability and stroke his own ego. Instead he concentrates on teaching young people how to play and how to compete. His teams have not always won the championship but he has yet to encounter a child that was not advanced by the experience of being under his coaching.

Coach Archie shares in this book his ideas about how coaches should coach. If all coaches adopted his approach and implemented his methods, I believe so many young people could be inspired to be successful constructive members of society. The lessons learned from the type of conditioning Coach Archie presents will equip young people to be able to be champions in life.

I would encourage you to read this book carefully because even if you are not a coach, you will still discover the power of loving influence. If we can all learn how to be a loving influence to others, it could literally change the world. One young person at a time, we can see millions of young people make a positive difference in the world. This book is not just about what Coach Archie does. It is about starting a movement that will get others involved in helping our young people.

Rev. Daniel T. Mangrum
Cornerstone Peaceful Bible Baptist Church

PREFACE

My coaching experiences and that of other coaches and parents has inspired me to write this book. My mission is simple. I want to bring awareness to coaches, parents, children and youth organizations. The substance of youth sports should be to build character, develop leaders, mentor, and coach, and teach discipline and respect through organized sports. My coaching philosophy--my message is *"It's not that serious. Have fun. Too much emphasis is placed on the actual act of participating in a sport and the wins and losses as opposed to developing youth and equipping them with life skills."* Coaches need to understand the power of influence we have over our youth athletes, and we should not take that for granted.

Coaches should seek kid's values.

Coaches and parents must lead by example.

TABLE OF CONTENTS

I Am a Youth Athlete

I am brave and strong and talented. But I'm still just a kid. I am not perfect. I am a work in progress. I need you to be patient while I test the limits of my body and work through the emotions that come with success and failure. When I make a mistake, I wonder if you'll be disappointed. When I reach my goals, I look to see if you are watching. I am a youth athlete. I love my sport. You call it competition. I call it playing the game. I want to win and have fun. I am a youth athlete. I am YOUR youth athlete. Winning feels great, but your praise feels infinitely better. Please remember these things, and I promise to do my best to make you proud.

Author Unknown

INTRODUCTION

The art of coaching youth (ages 14 and under) is to simply focus on teaching our youth, including how to lose with dignity and class, learn how not to get upset or mad and not think that winning is everything. I consider my style to be unique, and I have also been told by the parents of those participating in my programs that my style is unique. Children are brought up to think that winning is everything and that losing is not acceptable.

This is largely based on their parent's expectation. A youth athlete would do well if we would praise them for their good effort and refrain from criticizing them for their missteps. It is also important to allow the coach and the child to make the right connection. The more a parent yells at a child or coaches their child from the sidelines, the less effective the coach can be. What parents often don't realize is that you put your child in an awkward position due to the fact that they are not sure whom they should listen to. When being yelled at by a parent on the sidelines and also getting instruction from the coach, the children find themselves having to listen to someone, and that is more than likely going to be the parent. If the parent is calling for something that is contrary to what the coach is saying, then the child will be confused, and that becomes a problem.

I like for my players to take ownership of their team. I am here to teach them the game, but it is up to the team to perform what is being taught. I never say "my team," it is always "our team." And most importantly, the children are there to have fun, because after all, it's not that serious. Food for thought, if every coach were great, if every child was perfect, and every parent was committed, I wouldn't have to write this book. Here's a scenario, I hear parents, coaches and athletes complain all the time about what someone else did, and what they should have done. No matter what sport your child is participating in, think about this as well: if every athlete is in the right place at all times, and makes a good play every time, and never makes a mistake, every youth sporting event would end in a tie, and then what?

Hopefully after reading my book, everyone will take a different approach to youth sports and the growth of our STUDENT ATHLETES.

I hope you enjoy this book.

Chapter 1
THE MENTOR

ABOUT ME

I began participating in youth sports in the Police Boys and Girls Club in Washington, DC at the age of nine. The environment at the club was that of a safe haven for children with no drugs, no fights, no drinking and no profanity. The coaches and mentors were police officers. We were often reminded about the blue paddle, which was a long stick that the mentors and coaches used to put fear in us.

We never actually saw anyone getting hit with the paddle, but you knew it was there. The staff was very consistent with disciplining the youth. They taught us manners and demanded that we respect adults and our peers. I also participated in sports around other neighborhood recreation centers like Bald Eagle in Southwest, Washington. That is where I realized that a coach wasn't just a coach, given coaches like Coach Staggs, Coach Swann, Ms. Taylor and Ms. Spriggs. They were an extension of our parents, they would help with homework, give players rides home, and if you weren't doing the right thing, they would deal with that, too.

They also made sure that the sports we participated in were fun and fair. They would always ask how things were at home and in school. We would often walk to practice and when it was game time, we would pile into the coaches' cars and everyone would get dropped off individually afterwards.

I played basketball for St. Thomas Moore, which was a privilege.

That is where I had the pleasure of playing for Coach Allen who treated us as if we were his sons. He was the one that taught me how to support my entire team, not just the children that could play. Even though I often had the green light to shoot whenever I chose, I would always think about my teammates first. At St. Thomas Moore our team was successful in winning the Catholic Youth Organization (CYO) basketball championship two years in a row. Coach Allen never really raised his voice.

He would give us this look that would make us get it together real quick. Coach Allen's favorite phrase was "kick it," which meant just keep moving the ball and that is what we did each game. What's amazing to me is that those same principles apply today. I'm always telling my basketball teams that I coach to move the ball around constantly. Coach Allen also told us that once we got to high school, things would change, and change they did.

I was afforded the opportunity to attend Archbishop Carroll High School, which was one of the finest private schools in Washington, DC; it was here that I learned how to be independent and to understand the importance of being a mature, well-rounded young man. I had to work hard in the classroom while also competing in the various sports the school had to offer. I had the pleasure of playing basketball for Coach Barnes, track with Coach Bill Witte, and baseball with Coach Al Lucian. My football coaches were Coach Maus Collins, Coach Tim Breslin, and Coach John Badaczewski. At that time, Carroll was an all-boy's school, and we had some of the best talent in the DC, Maryland and Virginia area.

My high school coaches were firm but fair. They had a way of getting the best out of you. I can't repeat some of the things they would say, but how and when they would say things fit in at the right place and at the right time. My high school years went by so fast, and on my graduation day I reflected back on all my years as a child, and what jumped out the most were all of my coaches and how they all had such an impact on my life. I want to thank my mom and dad Clifton Beslow and Regina Beslow-Teague for always providing for me and instilling values in me that I still carry with me in my adult years. Mom and Dad, I love you both and thanks.

The next phase came at Morgan State University. I had no intention of furthering my athletic career in college, but that changed once I realized all the attention the college athletes received. Since I came from a high-profile high school, I was afforded the opportunity to play for the Morgan State Golden Bears football program. At Morgan, I learned the "wait your turn" process. No matter how good I may have thought I was, there was always an upper classmen to humble me, letting me know I had to pay my dues, like he had to pay his, and wait for the opportunity to compete. I was taught to be patient and to continue to work hard at Morgan State. I want to thank Coach Thomas, Coach Boyd and Coach Forrest for believing in me.

I grew up in Southeast Washington, D.C. At that time, things were far different than they are now in many respects. Both of my parents were hard workers and had little time to oversee my homework, come to my games or chauffeur me back and forth as parents do now. I came home from school to an empty apartment, did my homework unassisted and then went to the recreation center until it was time for my parents to come home. I played every sport I could think of and was very active. We didn't have video games, and there was little interest in television. The best way to spend time was to meet up with friends and engage in some sort of athletic activity.

I was a popular child, and as I look back on those years, I think it was because I wanted everyone to like me, and I always wanted to make people laugh. I still have these character traits, which is probably why I relate so well with the children. Despite the serious nature of my career day job as executive protection for a top city official, when I am not in that role, I seek to be very engaging and friendly.

All of the neighborhood children would compete in sports and playfully brag and have a lot of fun. While fights would occasionally break out, for the most part, we were all learning about healthy competition and striving to be the best.

I knew I was a little different from the other children, even at a young age. I would encourage and coach my peers and even older children. I would even offer words of wisdom, which the adults around me would marvel at because they did not know where I got the knowledge. I was trying to be the best that I could be, despite the distractions around me.

I think people liked me at that age because I was a motivator. I would always encourage the other children, offer suggestions and be friendly. I even remember trying to downplay the fact that I would score a point or beat another child. I didn't want others to feel bad if they lost. After all, it wasn't about winning or losing for me, it was about being in the game, doing the best we could do, and overall just having fun. I did have some children not look kindly upon me because I was always getting lots of awards and recognition, but at some point, I learned to not be bothered by those kinds of things. My mom would often say, "I don't know where he gets it from because neither I nor his dad was into sports."

Growing up, we lived for the opportunity to play sports and compete against each other, and the recreation center was our refuge. I was not discouraged or influenced by any negativity around me. I was aware but I was focused on doing well. By living in an urban area, there were many obstacles and situations that I had to cross and avoid. Many of my friends had the same opportunities I had, but they chose to go down a different path. Athletics and getting good grades kept me on the right track. I wasn't trying to be somebody that I wasn't. Others wanted to be the toughest dude in the neighborhood to get respect. I was popular because of how I conducted myself.

MY MOTIVATION TO START COACHING

I often reflect back to my childhood when athletics were popular but not as stressful as they are now. Young athletes are not given the chance to be self-driven, due to parental pressure, peer pressures and even the pressures imposed upon them by their coaches.

Let's start with my son Darius, who at the age of nine started playing football. Prior to football, he played basketball and tee ball and was pretty good at it all. When we tried flag football, we realized that he had something special going on. He was quick and could throw a football. When he started playing full contact football, I was skeptical. He was a quiet child, and he was the smallest child on the team. The first day of practice was uneventful. He showed no signs that this had been a bad idea, so I would monitor his progress over the next two months.

I did notice that he was still quiet and being unusually shy and he didn't seem to be having any FUN. I put the words in capital letters for a reason. The next day my son was finally given a chance to play. I was so excited and didn't know what to expect. As a proud Dad, I noticed the coach had placed my son in as a running back. When it was his first chance to run the ball, he didn't do well. Later in the game during the fourth quarter, he was given the chance to run the ball again. This time he took a pretty good hit and fumbled the ball. The other team recovered the ball and as my son was coming off of the field, you could see the tears in his eyes. All I could hear was his coach yelling to him at the top of his lungs saying: "Get off my field, and stop crying like a little girl! Stop being scared and soft! Don't put him back in the game." My insides were boiling, as he just demoralized my child in front of his peers, and he is only nine years old. What I noticed during my two-month observation period is that the children that could play, those that had the best talent, got all of the attention from the coach. The children with the least talent never got a chance to develop their skills.

I remember youth coaches that I had growing up as a child. All of them had similar qualities and they genuinely cared about each and every one of us. Not one time can I recall any of my coaches demoralizing me or anyone on the team. So I wondered whether I should say something to my son's coach or just bite my tongue. In the end, I became a coach not just for my son, but also for everyone's son and daughter.

I had another situation with my older son, Archie II, who at the time was 13. He played a little baseball and had a pretty decent bat, meaning he could hit a baseball very well. We tried football for two days, yes, just two days, and I realized early that football wasn't going to be his niche. So I signed Archie II up for basketball at the neighborhood recreation center. The first day of practice we arrived at the gym, and I noticed 15-20 children there with maybe three parents present. The boys were totally out of control. I told my son to have a seat until the coach arrived. Practice was supposed to start at 6 PM and end at 8 PM. It was now 6:45 PM and the coach arrives. He appears to be in his late 40's, not clean-shaven, with street clothes and not gym clothes on, no whistle and one basketball.

The children are wrestling, using profanity, boxing, just totally disrespectful towards the coach. So he says something to everyone in a whisper, and the children just ignore him. One of the dads yells as loud as he can, and the children just laugh. My son is still sitting at my side. It is now 7:15 PM and practice still has not started. Now, I have had enough with the horse playing, profanity and outright disrespect. I introduce myself to the coach and ask him if he needs help. With sweat running down his face and breath reeking of alcohol and cigarettes, I finally realized that this guy isn't even a coach. This is just some guy that took the job because no one else would. Now it's 7:45 PM with 15 minutes left, and nothing has been done. The boys come over and he introduces me as Coach Archie and they are told that I would be assisting him. So as we are leaving practice, several parents said, "Good luck!" For the next several practices, the head coach is a no-show. I told the director of the recreation center and was told that the head coach quit last week, and I was now the head coach. I smiled and said: "ok." My first official day as the head coach, I showed up to practice 30 minutes early. As the players arrived, I completed a roster, making sure that I had their parents' contact information. Then I respectfully asked the parents to wait outside of the gym during the first couple of weeks. That went over better than I thought; although the parents were still taking sneak peeks to make sure I wasn't harming their children.

My approach to coaching was never, and will never be, about the wins and losses. While I'm coaching on the youth level, my goal and vision is to build character in young men and young women. Once they reach high school and college, things may change because I know winning is important to those establishments. My reasoning for having closed practices was because I had to reach those young men first, not with jump shots, defenses, or offensive sets, but with real stories about my life. My first order of business was to cut the profanity. That took some strategizing. I told the players that as long as I am their coach, there will be no profanity when a woman, a parent or child is present. But any other time I will only allow for minimal outbursts based off of emotion. In a year, I took a winless team to the championship game. I received numerous praises from parents, other coaches and officials, stating that these young men needed me. That's why I love to coach.

My Reality Check

Early in my coaching career, another coach who asked me to be one of his assistants as an offensive coordinator approached me. I told him to let me think about it. I've heard stories about this particular coach and his approach to coaching, especially the fact that he shows favoritism towards his child. I'm the kind of person that doesn't get caught up in the rumor business. I never feed into the negative emotion of other people when they speak or say harsh things about coaches. Without going into a lot of details, I told the coach I would do it.

My first day at practice, I stood behind the scene just so that I could get a handle on the head coach's vision, demeanor and coaching style. So what I picked up on first was that the coach would get frustrated with the children often. As time went on, I settled into my position. The following statements I'm about to make really launched my coaching career. We had a football scrimmage set up. The team we scrimmaged turned out to be a little bigger than our team. On this day, they really got the best of us, meaning they were beating our children up pretty bad on the field. My son was playing quarterback and he was getting pretty banged up. Also, one of the other assistant coach's son played running back, and the opposing team was also hitting him hard.

On another play, the head coach's son was hit hard and the coach got upset and started yelling and fussing and said the scrimmage is over. Our head coach was in the middle of the field and was extremely upset. I was at a loss for words. I said to him, "Hold up, you want to stop the scrimmage because your child just got hit hard? My child has been getting hit all day." All of the parents were in an uproar with the actions that had just taken place on the field. At the end of the scrimmage, the head of the organization pulled the coaches to the sideline and simply said, "Coaches, we cannot have this kind of situation happen again.

The entire organization looks bad when a coach displays these kinds of actions." So the president of the organization says that he had to make some decisions going forward on how to provide a better football experience for the players and parents. He had been receiving a lot of complaints about this team. That's when I decided to speak up. I asked the president to give me a shot at turning things around for the team. I wanted to retain the current coaching staff, including the head coach. I was given the opportunity to turn things around and let me just say, that it was harder than I expected. This particular team had a franchise player whose parent was very vocal and influential in the organization. Whenever they spoke, the organization listened and responded. My philosophy was and has always been, to play all of my players often, no matter what their skill level. Needless to say, we weren't doing too well, and it wasn't long before the parents were voicing their concerns again.

One night I received a phone call from the president of the organization and a couple of his higher ups in the organization as well, that the complaints were still coming in and they offered to step in and assist me with coaching the team. Of course, I felt a certain way. You see I knew what the phone call was really about. It was about one player who they felt wasn't getting his due. The parent wanted all or most of my emphasis to be focused on that one player. During the conversation, I paused, and then I told the higher ups, I would rather step down all together. The problem I had about this issue was the focus on this child's ability as a football player but not the overall attitude towards the coaches, teammates and practice habits. By no means is this particular story meant to target a child or parent, but this is a formula for organizational issues and has also helped me to grow as a coach.

I've been around a lot of different head coaches; many of whom were tough, fun, teachers, egotistic, inexperienced, and the ones that would let you know their main purpose is about winning at all cause. They could care less about anything else, and that's based on their actions. As I stated in the past, I believe in youth sports. Youth sports to me are ages 14 and under. To me, it should be what I call the 90/10 rule. 90% fun for the children and 10% can be whatever the coach wants to get out of it. All of our efforts as coaches shouldn't be based on getting that win or a championship. I know a lot of my peers look at me crazy when I speak about not focusing on the winning aspect of coaching. By no means am I saying I'm not looking for a win or that I'm in it to lose. I'm in youth sports to coach, to mentor, to teach, build character, create leaders, and to put young ladies and young men in a position to be the best they can be. My success speaks for itself.

The purpose of this book is not to brag about my accomplishments. This book is to bring awareness to coaches that we need to unite and seek innovative ways to give these children all around life skills. The children that we are responsible for coaching, need more than just instruction on how to play the particular sport that they are involved in. Life as we know it now is going to be tough. As the years pass, things are going to be harder for our children to obtain and to achieve in order to maintain their livelihood. If they don't have their mental aspect in place they are going to lose a lot. Coaches need to rethink their focus.

A lot of coaches say they are mentors and they are here to help the children, but when you attend their practices, the message is contradicting. The focus is mainly on the outcome of the upcoming game, whereas if you're a good coach, that should be secondary. What you should attempt to do is coach the children on what happens before practice and what happens before a game. Also, let's do our part by ending practice on time, especially on school nights; work on having brief pre and post-practice talks, as well as pre- and post-game talks; and be mindful of the fact that the children and parents have been at the event for at least three hours and they are being kept there for 20 to 30 additional minutes, sometimes longer.

Coaches, stop talking just to hear yourself talk. Acknowledgement should be done after the game. Be sure to address criticism, which also has no place in youth sports, and any corrections or miscues that took place at your next practice and not after the game. Let's be respectful of the parents and children's time and also your own family's time.

MY COACHING PHILOSOPHY

The coach should not want the win more than the children. This should be obvious, but I have seen many coaches yell and punish the children when they don't win, even the parents. You should never get over excited or get mad at the children. When you model this behavior, it takes away from the whole experience and the children lose sight of what is important. When I have 25 different children on the team, I realize that I need to have 25 different expectations. Each has to be customized to the student athlete. I take the time to find out what each child wants out of the sport they are participating in. I go to their schools and talk to their teachers about their academic history. I combine both into the coaching experience. And it works magically for both boys and girls.

One of my top basketball players was a great athlete, but at the age of twelve he was quite a problem. He was a problem at home, at school and while participating in sports. At the end of the season, we were holding trials to build a new team and I didn't put him on the list. The other parents complained that I was making a bad decision to take this skilled player off the team and then also risk losing the team mom, also who, by the way, was exceptionally good at what she did with the teams administrative efforts. I took that risk. I told him and his mom that he could not return to play on my team until he got himself together.

Some time had passed, and I notified his mom to check out his progress to see if he could come back and play. His parents both agreed that he was ready. I told him that I was taking him back, not because he was one of the best on the team, but because I wanted others to learn that people can change. During his first game back, things were not going his way, he got fouled several times in the game, and I noticed his frustration. Even his father was noticing his frustration from the stands. He started to go back to his old ways and balled his fists because he was angry. I pulled him out and sat him down next to me on the bench, and I reminded him of our agreement. I told him this behavior is not acceptable on the court or in life. He made the adjustment and he has become a good student athlete whenever he's competing and even when he's not. To this day, his parents are glad to share his testimony and praise him on how he has changed.

I have come to realize over the years that my most effective method is to never yell at the children. They get chastised at home and at school, and they should never get chastised by the coaching staff or me. We as coaches should find strategies to get our points across. Through the years I have seen and heard many coaches yell profanity at the children. It is absolutely not acceptable or appropriate. After all, this is all about recreation and is intended to get them away from their pressures and stress. I was asked by a coach why I get 100% turnout at my practices. My response to him was, my players understand that I care. I'm quite sure all coaches care about their athletes. But what I do is make sure all the children are having a good experience, whether it is at practice or an actual game. They have fun from the moment they get out of the car, during practice and when they are leaving. I want it to be fun for them.

Children may shut down if you chastise them. We need to let them know that they are not going to school to impress mom, dad, me or whoever; let's emphasize that they go so they can have a productive life as they go into their adult years. We need to express this more. We have to remove ourselves from the equation as parents. Just reiterate the real meaning for going to school. Now there are times when a particular athlete may do something because they are being lazy. Then I address it accordingly. All children are not the same. Their personalities and expectations and goals are different. As a coach, I need to tap into all of their goals, expectations, wants and needs. Many of the children may not want to continue to play sports. They may just want to be a part of something or want to spend time with their best friend, or do what their parents may have done. Allow the children to make the decision for themselves. My youngest son Jordan, for example, was ranked in the country for the 100-yard dash and so was his relay team. He had reached a point in his life, and he decided not to run track anymore. I had mixed emotions because I knew he could be a great track and field guy. I thought that he was discouraged because children were getting taller, and he could not dominate like he used too. I was looking at it as if he was quitting, so I had to check myself. When he participated he was giving 110% so I had to respect his wishes.

So he decided to play baseball, and he actually did well. He turned out to be a good outfielder, due to his speed and athleticism, but he couldn't quite get his hitting straight, I explained to him, that with hard work and determination, his hitting would come around. My point - try to allow the student athlete to make his or her own decisions. When it comes to their athletic decision, the field of sports is truly a good way to teach a child responsibility and ownership. I always want to get involved in the academic lives of the children and their mindsets, so I asked the parents for permission to visit their schools to get them back on track. I visit as many schools as I can, and you should have seen the expressions on the child's faces. They were in awe that their coach would spend the entire day in their classroom and pay attention to the curriculum. The children were excited.

You would think that all parents would be grateful knowing that their children's coach goes the extra mile to make sure that their children get more from their youth sports experience than just what goes on in practice and at the games. I would hear things like, "you have non-coaching skills." So I would like to say to that very small percentage of people, instead of bashing me amongst their peers or behind my back, you need to focus on the bigger picture--how someone like myself is your child's mentor who's always checking on their homework, and getting into their heads and finding out what is going on in their lives. I have a way of reaching the children, and I know this is what God intended for me to do. I don't think I deserve to get negative feedback. For example, during basketball season, I would hear complaints like, why didn't I play a

2-3 defense, or why didn't I run a certain play. But it doesn't matter if your child is making bad passes or ill-advised shots or getting an attitude on the court. You are only paying attention to the results of the game, not the behavior of the child, so the child then thinks it is acceptable. I do not think it is acceptable. Parents get so consumed by the game that they don't see their children saying curse words or swelling up or balling their fists.

Parents will turn a deaf ear to their children cursing. It is not my job to discipline a child on behavioral skills. I can talk to them or console them or tell them what the expectation is on my team, but the other part is the parent's job. The buzz would also be that I am a good coach starting out--academics first and athletics second. You would not believe the number of parents that don't support that philosophy. Their main focus is wins, and they put that same pressure on the children. That year forced me to give up basketball temporarily. If I do decide to go back, I will work with younger children, ages 6 – 10 who appreciate getting taught. If they are not disciplined and used to getting the proper tutelage, it is a disaster when they get to the 12- and 13-year-old age group.

When I coached basketball, I had a startup team. When I acquired my team, all the other AAU teams were already formed, so I had to build my team from scratch with children that were eager to play but did not have the experience in playing. My job is to teach the fundamental skills, and in many instances a lot of our youth do not have those skills. My message and motivation is to mentor young men and women to get them on the right track for life. Not to get them on the right track just to win championships. Parents don't pay enough attention to that.

I started out with a mediocre team. We were doing okay. The first year we won our regional championship with a bunch of guys that people did not expect to win. Through hard work and a lot of effort, we stuck together and the guys pulled it through. The following year, trying to go forward in the direction that the organization was going, my job was to get good children that wanted to learn but could play on a competitive level. Those components are hard to find at the age 13 because at that age many of those children are stubborn and stuck in their own ways. I reached out to a couple of children I knew and I advised them that if they knew of any other parents that wanted to bring children out, they could pass it on. By doing this, I acquired three decent ball players. These particular children came from established organizations or teams. The teams they were on had five or six children that could play and these children had parents that complained about playing time the coach showing favoritism, the coach did not like their child, the coach did not know what he was doing, the coach yelled too much.

There was always an excuse for these players. For me, I did not care if the child was a problem with other coaches because I always felt that I could work with any child, particularly as the season went on. Some parents fail to realize that they play a major role in their child's success on and off the court. Their reactions in various situations can teach children positive or negative behaviors that can either help the child or put them at a disadvantage. It is ideal for parents, teachers, coaches and others to work together as a united front and provide consistent teachings to children. As I continue, I will give a few personal examples of how discord between parents and coaches has affected the performance of some of my athletes and explain what we could do better.

One area that suffers is a child's self-awareness. In the highly competitive league of AAU basketball, children consistently play at an exceptionally high level. As they train and compete against other top athletes, their shortcomings are exposed and talents are highlighted. Originally, students playing in this league were selected based on their talent level, but in recent years, it has become flooded with many players that are not at the skill level that this program was intended for. One major reason for this is the parents. Due to the respected reputation of the AAU league, some parents strongly desire to have their child take part in it but unfortunately these parents have a very distorted view of the child's actual skill level. In many cases, they will go to extreme lengths to get their child in the league even if it means creating an entirely new team. Parents, this is a decision that not only affects your child but others around them. By flooding the program with children that are not at the appropriate skill level, the challenging nature of the entire league decreases and players aren't pushed competitively. How can the players improve if they are not clear about their current skill level? Parents and coaches should work together to determine the best team or league for each child, letting go of all biases and earnestly evaluating the child on their talent and potential.

Players should always give 100% of themselves during a game. Work ethic is very important. Players should not slack off because they think something is below them. Coaches can only do so much. They give the player the tools they need to be successful and then it's up to the player to put it into action. There once were some highly skilled players that came to my team because they wanted to work with me as their coach. These children had behavioral problems, were lazy and made every excuse to quit.

When game time came, we were playing teams that we knew were at lower skill levels than these guys, but they did not put forth the effort necessary to win the game. We lost. Never underestimate your opponent because the children you play against want to win as much as you do and are willing to put in the work to make it happen. In everything, you must put your best foot forward. Oftentimes you get out what you put in, and if you do not make an effort to reach your goal, then you can't be surprised when you don't achieve it.

Commitment is another area that can suffer if parents aren't careful. It is not unusual for certain children to go from team to team hoping to eventually stumble upon the next big thing. Parents will pull their child from one team and place them on another, expecting different results. They will never be satisfied because it will still be the same parent, same child and same skill level. The parent may place them on a team that is more successful and has a better record with hopes that they will get more playing time or perhaps benefit in some way from being a part of the team. You may take them to a team that is more successful and has a better record but keep in mind that if the child is not playing at the necessary skill level they will not get playing time because the coach of the new team will want to maintain their winning record; and then what? Would it be best to move the child again until you find a team that is both successful and will give the child playing time? Bad move.

You must teach the player commitment. Teach them how to win and how to lose. Through hard work, practicing on practices and listening to instructions from their coach, they will gain the skills and learn the plays needed to be successful. This does not happen overnight, but if the child is taught to stick with it and to continue giving 100%, they will see growth within themselves and with the team overall.

Finally we have motivation and encouragement. What ever happened to "for the love of the game?" This applies to parents, players and coaches. I had a really tall child on my team who played at a very low skill level. He was a great child but he didn't want to be a player and never really progressed. His parents and those in the basketball community saw a big child and decided for him that basketball is where he would excel. He was recruited off of my team and ultimately it was realized that he did not have the skill set and did not get any playing time. He lost his excitement and love of the game and no longer found it enjoyable.

Stop pressuring children to play in order to get scholarships because you can't afford to send them to college. What type of message are we sending them? Parents attempt to coach from the stands, screaming out orders and expressing their disappointment in a manner that does not help the player. Cursing out the child will not make them play better. It will only serve to discourage them and add more pressure. It feeds negative energy into the child and that will stick with them for the rest of the game and possibly off of the court. Americans have taught their children that they must excel in sports in order to go to college. That is way too much pressure for young athletes, especially those in eighth grade and below. When children go to high school and college, the coaches are focused on keeping their jobs, so you do not know how or what they will provide for your child because the focus is on them.

It seems like everyone has selfish motives. This mindset is completely different from volunteer coaches. We don't get paid for anything. We give up our time and energy for your child and deal with shortcomings, behavioral problems and varying skill sets to teach them the game. We do this not because we have something to gain. A coach's focus should be on the all-around growth of a player. My players were excited about me coming to their schools. I encouraged them to improve their grades, turn in their homework, and strive to be better students and also to want this for themselves. I do this on my own, voluntarily. I want to trigger something in the minds of my players not only about their athletics but also about their academics, helping them to grow not only as a player but also as a person.

I've given all of those examples simply to emphasize the importance of parents and coaches communicating and working together. At the end of the day, we all want the same thing: to provide our children the best opportunities that will allow them to be the best they can be.

STRATEGIES

If you put ten children together and ask them about their parents' expectations about what they need to do to go to college, 9 out of 10 say an athletic scholarship, which is not fair. It is a subliminal message that keeps on getting repeated. If they fail on the athletic field, they consider themselves a failure. We should not equate athletics to school. We should encourage school first and then athletics; if you get A's and B's, then you can play sports. We need to focus on the books and studying and how important good grades are to allow them to get scholarships. Way more youth go to college on academic scholarships than on athletic scholarships, so putting that pressure on a young child makes them almost destined to fail.

I do a lot of hugging. I shake their hands. I speak to them. I coach and mentor all the children. I don't do it to impress parents or organizations. I'm just trying to reach a child to give them a force to drive themselves and achieve everything they attempt to do in life. Every year, I have children that come to my teams based on my reputation over the years. I have had children coming from broken homes, some have wanted to commit suicide, and others are truant and have behavioral problems. They have all come through the organization. By the grace of God, when they leave, they are a different child. I change their minds, their attitudes, and their perspective on learning. I have a way of getting into their heads and explaining why they should not do what they may be doing, and I relate it to my own life. We have to find strategies and tactics to reach the children to help them be successful.

A parent called me one day because the child was feeling pressure on what high school to choose. The child is athletic and tall for his age. I told the mother he should not have so much pressure as an eighth grader. He started crying and was upset because he did not want to let anyone down. Our parents think that the children must get scholarships so the parent doesn't have to pay for school. We need to motivate the children to do well in academics and the scholarships will fall into place with this strategy. The eighth grader is twelve and turning thirteen and it is too much pressure and the parents must realize that his mentality at this stage does not allow him to make this kind of adult decision. Parents need to stop forcing the children to be top athletes, to be perfect, whether it is for a teen pageant, sports or anything. You can push and motivate them, but know their limits.

Parents and coaches need to reemphasize to the children that failure is not always a bad thing. If you fail it also helps you grow. It forces you to challenge yourself to be better. The next boy or girl is trying also, and maybe you can do more the next day. Learn to teach your children how to fail. One weekend I on purpose lost the game. I am not your typical coach. In losing the game, we dropped from 2nd to 8th place in state rankings. At the end of the game, none of the children showed sadness or had their heads down. The after game celebration was louder than the pre-game celebration. Others looked at us and wondered if we realized we lost. The children mirror the image of the coach.

Coaches need to realize that the children mirror your image so you must be careful about how you come across to the children. You couldn't even realize that my children lost the football game. Of course the parents had a whole host of suggestions as to what we could have done differently. You shouldn't care about the win as a parent or even as a coach. You must care more about getting the child set up to succeed and win in life. I have witnessed coaches calling the parents that have disciplined their children and kept them home from practice saying, "Children make mistakes, but I need him out on the field." What is that about? Instead figure out why the child is messing up in school or being disrespectful to his parents. Forget about making the team look good. What is that showing the child?

READB4CONTACT

There are several things that I do before practicing or playing a game. We ReadB4Contact and we pray. The opportunity to read not only allows all of my players to remember the importance of academics and to expand their minds and possibilities, it also affords those not as athletically inclined to shine when they read out loud or discuss their readings.

The purpose of the ReadB4 Contact program is to bridge the gap between the most talented athletes and those that are less talented. After observing the children for some years, I figured what better way to let that happen than academics. For example, the most talented child may not be the most talented academically and vice versa. So before practice, I have those that are academically talented stand before teammates and tell them what they have read. This process builds character, builds leadership and incorporates fun into learning. I let them laugh and make jokes as long as they are not disrespectful to others. All team members must give them their undivided attention. I have some children that have A's, but on the field they lack confidence.

This program allows this young lady or man to speak about something that they are confident in, and it gives them an opportunity to shine. If, for example, Steve cannot block, run, tackle shoot jump shots or run very fast, but is very articulate and reads very well, their academic confidence at this point allows them to shine in front of their teammates. The top athletes then look at Steve in a different light. When you put two children together, they can teach each other better. They can teach each other Algebra, for example, better than adults, so that is the way of bridging the gap between athletics and sports while coaching the children. When I tell them to bring a book, all the children get excited. They really do look forward to the program. It gives them a chance to unwind from school and the books the children pick up are very interesting. You can pick up on their personalities based on the materials they choose to read about and what keeps their interest. It is up to me to peak their interest even further. The program just broadens their horizons and lets them know that it is cool to read. If I reiterate to them later about reading, they are more apt to do it because it was implemented in our practice.

I did a ReadB4Contact event where I had the football team with 11- or 12-year-olds bringing whatever book they wanted to bring and then reading for 20 minutes. After they read, I asked them to stand up and talk about what they read. 100% of the children brought books and were excited about participating. The program is really important. They should not come to practice and do it as punishment, even if you do group homework before practice. It builds camaraderie, public speaking skills and erases shyness. Some children articulate better than others.

Some are known to be shy and spoke about their books, and it is a win/win situation. The purpose is to build character--not focus on wins or loses--just build character and create leaders. Coaches and parents walk by in amazement that the children are reading the books. Parents take pictures and other children run past while running their laps and asking why they read books at football practice. My children get locked in and focused on it, and this is one of the many things I do to get the message across, focusing on the individual student athlete and scholar and teaching them that school and respect come first before scoring a touchdown or winning a diving contest.

The other thing I do is pray before and after practice. I ask all of the team members at a certain time to lead the prayer. It is amazing to see how this practice calms things down, puts the players in a better, more positive mental place. Even the parents are amazed when they witness their children praying. When we are ready to depart, we pray again, the parents can also join in. We leave the practice or game with a sense of calm and positivity that we can take with us. Prayer provides a calming and soothing effect on our players as individuals and as a team.

I also don't have my football players doing a lot of hitting drills, whereas a lot of coaches do without realizing the true and cause and effect. I look at it this way. There are two types of football players, those that like to hit and those that don't. There is no middle ground. I conduct a lot of form tackling and low-impact to prevent from discouraging children that don't like a lot of contact.

CLASS VISITS

The Process: I ask my parents about their child's school and classroom status. I'm not only looking at or checking on the children that aren't doing well, but those that are excelling as well, such as your honor roll students. Also those children that are improving on their own, as well as those children whose parents had to utilize certain strategies to get them back on point. I would call the parents or ask them on the practice field, if they have any concerns about their children as it relates to his or her academics, then I would proceed to tell them that I do school visits. My school visits consist of monitoring my players' behavior, their teacher's demeanor and all of their classmates, especially the ones they share the same desk with.

Now, of course, while I'm in the classroom, my players are normally on their best behavior, which is cool because that lets the teacher know that the child is respectful. Upon my arrival to the school I would check in with the principal's office to make sure I get the players class schedules and a layout or diagram for the school, if time permits. I would introduce myself to the players' guidance counselor and the school principal. My attire consists of khaki pants or sweats and a clean, pressed coach's shirt with my name on it.

My parents' responsibility is to notify the school that I'm coming via phone call and email, stating my purpose for the visit. So, now back to the classroom. As I was saying, I would make sure my players participate in class discussions, pay full attention to the teacher or whomever is speaking in front of the classroom, make sure players are dressed appropriately and have good body posture while sitting at their desks and that they are not talking to their classmates. I usually text parents while I'm observing their children to make sure I don't forget any important information like quizzes, projects, homework assignments, after school tutoring and detention. I also recommend to teachers to switch my players to certain desks, based on my observation, not theirs. I also check the teacher's body language, how well prepared they are, their patience, classroom structure and how well they keep the children's interest.

One day, I was in one of my players' science classes and the teacher had mentioned several times throughout the class that she would be conducting tutoring after school for anyone that wants to attend. I looked at my player and gestured to him that he will be attending. When class was over, I said, "Stephen don't forget about going to tutoring," then he said, "Coach, I have to check with my mom," and I told him that I already took care of the notification to his mom. He smiled and said, "Okay coach, see you at practice." So I told him that he wouldn't be attending practice that evening since he had to study for two quizzes and start a project for the next day.

The majority of my parents love this process, while some parents normally the dads, seem to show resistance. I explain to both parents that my purpose is for us to be bookends to their child and for me to reiterate to their child the things that they are already telling them. I also explain to my parents that peer pressure plays a big part in a child's life. If we team up to help the child, that's a formula for success.

By no means am I trying to replace anyone's parents. I added this chapter to this book because I think school visits by coaches on the youth level speak volumes for the coach and the organization that is being represented. I'm sure this will catch on. I'm not saying I'm the only coach that does this, all I know is I've never seen it done. Coaches, children look up to us and we have the power and the ability to change a young lady or young man's life, as it relates to their academics, early and we need to stress respect to our children. They must respect God or whatever form of religion they practice, first. Respect mom and dad; respect themselves, and everyone else they come in contact with. The school visit could really become a reality TV show.

While I'm in the classroom, these are some of the things I witness. The 6th graders, 7th graders and 8th graders all use profanity at some point during the class. The students are also doing hand gestures. This is all going on while the teacher is trying to teach. Let me give you some actual classroom events. I can recall on one school visit, the teacher advised the students that they were going to change work groups in an attempt to break up students who sit together because they are friends, or had a negative influence on their classmates. While the teacher was trying to calm the class down before she put the names up on the power point, she wanted order in her classroom. Mind you, after multiple threats to punish certain children, which had no effect on calming the children down, she proceeded to place the names on the board.

Okay, you know some power point takes a while to come up on the screen, as the different groups started to appear, the class became unruly with very crude language, and this is a 7th grade class. I'm not sitting with that. The "B word" was used several times and this is coming from a couple of young ladies. The young men were twice as bad. After about 10-15 minutes of the class saying how they are not going to follow the teacher's instruction, the teacher finally conceded defeat and said we will try this another day. There was one particular young lady who was asked to go sit with a group of three young ladies, and she said, "'F that, I'm not moving. They need to come over here." The teacher asked the young lady kindly if she would move, and once again, the young lady said, "F no. I'm not moving."

Ok, this particular class visit wasn't all bad. Prior to walking into this same disruptive classroom, one of my football players was engaged in conversation while the teacher was talking. When I walked into the classroom, I introduced myself and I told the teacher I was there to do an observation of one of my football players. I told her I was his coach and mentor. My player looked up, and if you could have seen the look on his face. It was priceless. So, meanwhile, the young man that was sitting beside him was still talking. Then he realized that my player had gone into respect coach Archie mode. So the child kept talking and trying to force my player to talk when they both knew it wasn't the right time to talk while the teacher was giving instructions.

So, while my player remained focused, the other child continued to talk and he obviously had no intention on trying to learn anything on that day. The teacher gave out instructions for the students as to what she expected of them for the remainder of the class time. Well, needless to say, my player finished the first task and his friend was still sitting there talking and not writing anything, not listening and just clowning the whole time. So then came the moment that made me proud and put all my class visits in perspective. The teacher put a time limit on the last assignment and my player was the first to complete it. She rewarded him with an "A" just for completing it because no one else in the class came close to completing the assignment.

The teacher made it a point to let the class know that someone had completed the assignment ahead of the allotted time, so there is no reason no one else was not done. The class was trying to figure who had finished, so when the teacher said who it was, she had a smile on her face, and the students started giving my player his props. Prior to the bell sounding to change classes, I walked over to my player and simply asked him how it felt after getting all the praise and love from his teacher and classmates for that small but huge accomplishment. The reason why I say small initially is because he only did what he was supposed to do. And the thing that made it huge was the young man hadn't been doing anything, so to show his teacher and his peers what he is capable of doing academically was priceless.

These are some of the tools and strategies I use after my class visits. I'm able to articulate to my players that the same attention they are seeking by not doing what they are supposed to do in school will double in impressing your peers by doing the right thing. I also stress to my players to lead by example so that they can make a difference in their own life, as well as helping their friends to achieve success by doing what's required of them in school.

So why do I do school visits? I do school visits because my players respect me. I do school visits because I care. I do school visits because our youth are struggling. I do school visits for single parents that don't have the time to do them. I do school visits because I know how much influence I have as a coach. Coaching is my vehicle that gets me into the schools, homes and minds of young athletes to force change and encourage progress. I want to take this time to personally thank all teachers and administrators for what you do. One final thought, I encourage parents and teachers to tell our youth to say these three words before they enter their schools each day and for the rest of their education. Simply say "I Need This!"

The Essay by Braedon J Domino

Coach Archie

The African-American that has influenced me to further my education is Archie R. Beslow also known as "Coach Archie". Having him in my life is such a blessing. I can honestly say that because of the time and effort he has spent making sure I was doing well not only on the football field, but more importantly in school and life all together, that I have become the person I am now. Since the day that I overheard someone speak on behalf of his character, I was not only impressed but interested with the things I was hearing. I had learned that you cannot always make a judgment on someone you have never met before, but surely when I was introduced to him there was no doubt in my mind that everything that was said about this man was true to the last detail. Before I met Mr. Beslow I was a typical 5th grader, I didn't really think school had much of a meaning or served any type of purpose other than to keep children occupied until their parents returned from work and school couldn't really get me anywhere.

I thought to myself, "What's the point of school? I will never even use this stuff!" After having just one talk with him he not only opened my eyes to the reality of life, but he gave me new perspective about school and how to approach things. He told me to think about my report card like a paycheck. He said, "Just like you get A's and B's on your report card, you get A's and B's in Life. Treat school like your job and you have to continuously push yourself to the limit to do well and get that paycheck. What you do now serves as the deciding factor for the rest of your life". I took those words to heart and I will never forget them. It's definitely something I'll share with my future children. Coach Archie is more than just a mentor, he is a father figure as well. He taught me so much about what it takes to get along in life and the topic that would pop up in almost every conversation was something having to do with the importance of education. Sometimes I'd look at him like he was crazy and say, "

Coach we're at football practice remember?" and he'd look at me, grin, and then continue talking about school. He defines the word "man" in every way shape and form. His wisdom and understanding helped me to develop a great work ethic. He helped me learn from my mistakes of his own and he has shown me how to avoid them. Because of him I've learned that in order to do exceptionally well you need to first recognize the things that cause you to fail and then get rid of those distraction and temptations. Those temptations are the things that blind you and haze your vision so you aren't able to see what it is that will allow you to thrive. By blocking those distractions and temptations you are then able to see things in a different light and you can realize that certain factors need to change to better yourself. He has influenced me to seek the truth.

Because of him I will strive to achieve clarity of my thoughts, nobility of character and purity of heart; therefore, I will pursue my education with and honor. Embracing excellence and renouncing mediocrity. I will assume responsibility for my actions and I will never settle for what will just get me by. I will try to follow in his footsteps and help others see all the great places education can take you by exemplifying what it means to be an outstanding student. Coach Archie has engraved within my mind that without knowledge you cannot prosper. In the world we live in today you are always competing with someone, just like in sports. The only advantage that you can have over the other person is intelligence and will power.

If you don't have either than you won't be successful in life. In the 2010-11 season Coach Archie did something that blew the minds of many. Right after our games he said that from that day forth every Monday from 6:30-7:00 we would read and after reading we would have to give a short summary to the team about the book we had read. Later, that turned into him giving us homework. He told us to write out summaries almost like book reports. The rule was if the homework wasn't done then that player didn't play on Saturday. He called this his "Read Before Contact" project. At first a lot of the players didn't take him seriously, but if you know Coach Archie you know that: 1) he is true to his word and 2) he takes education more seriously than he does football. So the players sat out and that gave them the motivation to do their work instead of being bench warmers and water boys. This continued from then to this day. Another thing that he does is school visits. He will pop up at any given time when you least expect it just because he cares enough to check up on his team to make sure that they are doing everything that needs to be done in the classroom and if that's not the case he deals with you at practice. He was always fair when giving out punishments to the team. The man really turned the worst students into some of the top ones and not that but he kept them out of trouble as he did so. He is not only a coach, but he protects the Mayor of D.C., Mayor Vincent C Gray.

Hearing some of the stories he has told the team made me want to do the same so ever since then I've wanted to be a United States Marshall. This would be my way of giving back and serving others. To say the least he has inspired the minds of all of those that he has come into contact with. I am one of many that he has influenced and I could never forget the vital and useful advice that he has shared with me over the years. He has touched the hearts of countless people in numerous ways and I know I will keep him in my life forever. I prayed every night for some type of inspiration, some type of miraculous human being that will help bring the world to love and stomp out ignorance and hatred. I can certainly say that God has answered my prayers and I'm sure the prayers of scores of people. I owe it all to him. I use to just settle for B's on my report card and I looked at a B as fine with me or I'd even say to myself, "Well, at least it's not a C". Now every quarter I strive for straight A's.

Thanks to Coach Archie I set goals for myself and the bar is always set high. I have learned how to manage my time and be discipline when it came to getting assignments finished and being able to put the phone away for a while. This has helped me to isolate myself from distractions and stay focused on getting work done instead of procrastinating and just blowing work off. Before meeting him I never had bad grades, but they were never off the charts and now I do the utmost best to get those kinds of grades. I believe everyone is fully able to get those off the chart grades if you really take school serious as if it was to be their only lifeline, which it is. He always said that we shouldn't just do well in school for our parents, but do it instead for yourself because at the end of the day it's your life that is hanging in the balance so take pride in your school work. As I think it is appalling that we have such low test scores and yet we still deem ourselves as the most powerful country on the entire planet. What is power and authority without having any notion at all what to do with it? We might as well not have that power at all. We need more people who recognize the importance of going to school and getting their education because that is the only way our future will be bright. The children of the present are the minds that will shape the future. Coach Archie has made sure that the children he has come into contact with will restore hope to the human race.

"Education is our passport to the future, for tomorrow belongs to the people who prepare for it today." - Malcolm X.

Chapter 2
THE PARENT

The definition of a parent is a father or mother, a parent acting as a father or mother, also a protector or guardian. I wanted to start this chapter off with the definition of a parent so that we all can be clear of the meaning. The topics, issues, concerns, complaints, misunderstanding, etc., that I will speak on are to let you know that I, too, was a parent that complained. I had issues with my son's playing time. I was the negative parent in the stands. However, staying for my son's practice was a must for me and I will explain that later. I was a parent of the "not enough group."

These are parents that no matter how hard their child practices or plays, it just isn't enough. I was also that parent that would talk to my child the entire ride going to the game about what he needs to do and how to do it. I also couldn't wait to get back in the car so that during the ride home I could tell him what he did wrong and what he should have done. I later learned that this type of behavior wasn't effective for the growth of my children. So that's my introduction to the parent section of this book.

Now let's get down to business. By no means am I trying to degrade, belittle, bash or say that some parents are bad parents. That is not my intention or my purpose. My purpose is to bring awareness to both parents and coaches. The complaining parent is usually a parent that doesn't have all the facts or information he or she needs at the start of any season, so they have to go by what they see or hear from other parents. We all know what happens when parents talk amongst one another. The story changes from parent to parent, and it's usually a lot of speculation involved. So I encourage parents to ask questions and hold the coaches, organization leaders and athletic directors accountable for their child's success while competing in youth sports.

As a parent, ask the coach what his mission or vision is for his team, your child and the organization. Before you complain, attend meetings, make suggestions, volunteer your time, and display a positive image. With these simple things your complaints may disappear. Also, try not to complain around your child because this will affect the respect level your child has for his or her coach. Parents often times complain about their child's playing time, which in a lot of cases should be a valid complaint. Not to mention, there is a fee involved in youth sports to participate, gas prices are soaring and people's time is valuable, and no one wants to waste their time in the first place, which brings me back to parents complaining about playing time. This is the point where communication plays a major role.

You as a parent have every right to ask about your child's playing time. Whenever you spend money, you should expect to get your money's worth, and at the end of the day, you should be provided with good service from the organization, team administration and coaches. As a parent, you should request updates on your child's progress. Also evaluate your child's progress yourself. Let me give you a hint. The most important thing to look for is to see if your child is having fun, and if he or she is, then please leave your complaints in the car.

Youth sports should be an outlet for children and not another stressful adult-driven situation like home and school responsibilities. Ensure the child gets what he or she wants out of the experience based on their timetable and not the adults. This means, don't force or put pressure on your child to become an instant success, but allow your child to grow or progress according to the child's skill level. And don't measure his or her skill based on someone else. If you really think about it, the average child is shy, and while participating in youth sports, the child's talents will always be exposed whether their talent is good or bad. We as parents need to base a child's progress on his or her personality. If a child is passive or timid, then the progress may take longer. If a child is aggressive, then the process tends to happen quicker. The process meaning, the final product where the child was when they started and how they're progressing during the season and where they ended up. Before you complain about playing time, I hope you will take my advice or at least consider what I'm saying.

Over my years of coaching, I have come across many families with more than one child on a team. There have been instances where in one family, the parents and a number of their children are all athletic, with the exception of one child. I have seen parents try to force this child to perform and to be just as good an athlete, or better, when in fact the child does not have the genetics or athletic ability to be as good a player as the parent(s) would like them to be. I have a child now that is just not a football player. He is doing the best he can. But certain parents want to put them in the situation they may have had, like being a quarterback like the parent was as a child. Or a running back--a high profile position when the child doesn't have the athletic skills or even desire.

You need to find out from your child what they want out of the particular sport. Find out what they want, not what you want. If the child says they just want to be on the team, then allow that. The child may wind up being a coach and not a player. No child should be pressured in athletic sports. At all times, the children should be having fun. When my sons were playing sports if they wanted to talk I would. If they want your feedback, then give it, but if you quickly start providing feedback, particularly negative, then it is not a positive exchange.

Parents, we need to start making our children's small accomplishments large. For example, if a child gets all A's that's a big deal, which for all intents and purposes it is, and the child should be rewarded. So how about that child that usually averages a low C and a D, but somehow he manages to get an A somewhere on his report card. I think that should be celebrated as well. Let me give you a couple more examples. On average, PTA meetings aren't attended in large numbers. PTA in my city stands for Parent Teacher Association, which is now called PTSA (Parent Teacher Student Association) in some school systems.

I agree with this change to PTSA. I understand that our work schedules are hectic, and some families have multiple jobs and there are some parents without support systems. Let me suggest this, meetings related to the growth of your child should be attended. If you can't make it, then it is your obligation to find someone that can make it--a grandparent, other relative, friend or even your child's coach. Also speaking on accomplishments, if your child receives any kind of award or recognition, it should be treated just like we do sporting events and invite the same people that you would invite to any youth sporting event for your child.

If your child is receiving a perfect attendance award, the auditorium should be filled with relatives and friends. If your child is competing in a science fair, multiple family and friends should attend. Anything that your child receives or participates in that's positive, he or she should have an audience just like or larger than the support that you get at a youth sporting event.

So let's go back to the PTSA meetings. Make sure your child is present with you or whoever will be attending in your place. And do the best you can to leave attitudes or any negative vibes or spirits in the car. By keeping things calm and you showing a positive demeanor, the child will feel comfortable, and with calm in the room, your brain will be allowed to function properly, meaning stress and anger won't be allowed to take over your questions and block the chance of finding resolution. I encourage parents to do observation visits at your child's school and don't visit only when your child is not doing well. We need to visit even when they're doing great. This gives you a chance to monitor their surroundings as well and to see who has an influence on your child. And like I have said in the previous section, this will serve as good reference for you to have dialogue with your child.

PARENTS AND FANS IN THE STANDS

What is he doing? Why do they have practice again today? I'm taking my child off the team! He can't coach! He plays his child all of the time! Shoot the ball. Don't pass the ball. The referee is cheating! Put my child in the game! Why is that child in the game? To add to all of this, there are those occasional outbursts of profanity. There is no place for this type of conduct in youth sports, or any level of sports, for that matter. My focus is youth sports. As you well know, if the coaches can hear all of this, guess what, the children that are participating can also hear it.

This is huge contradiction in the way that we are raising and teaching our children. We should be teaching respect, humility, discipline, politeness, etc. And please refrain from the confrontations with the opposing team fans. But yet, in the heat of a battle or youth athletic event, the adults just lose it. If you as an adult can lose it, what do you think your child is going to do?

The key word for youth sports is fun, which is broken down from the word fundamentals. If the coach focuses on making each practice and game fun, then the mental aspect will take care of itself. If a child is having fun, you can work on their mental state as far as behavioral skills, manners, work ethics and education. As a fan or supporting parent, family member or friend, the only thing that should come from the fans in the stands is encouragement. That's it and that's all. You have to be mindful of the negative energy that can transcend from the stands to the players and coaches. Also the coaching staff volunteer their time for your child. That alone should merit only encouraging words from the stands.

I can recall one of my football games, it was the Maryland State Championships, it was a first-round game and the team we played had a young man that played running back. He totally dominated the game on both sides of the ball. Needless to say, we lost. Usually, I block the fans out, but on this particular night something came over me. I had had enough. You see, our team had accomplished so much already in the season that I couldn't understand where all of the negativity was coming from.

Normally, there are always a couple of folks that no matter win or lose, there is an issue. After the game, I brought the team together to commend them on their efforts, and I explained to them that they could not win them all. Then I directed my comments to the parents, stepparents, grandparents, sisters, brothers, and friends. While trying to keep my composure, I said to all that were present, as much as I do for these children on a daily basis outside of just being their coach, I shouldn't have to hear anything negative coming from our fans because I have feelings too. For those of you who are aware of the sacrifices made by the coaching staff, you should have stepped in and diffused the negativity and explain to the person or persons what this coaching staff and team is all about.

So I left them with this: please don't criticize me when I lose and tell me what I have done because that game is history. But I do welcome you coming to me with something positive or negative when you're in a good mood as opposed to a bad one. Believe me, the same mistakes I made during that lost, I've also made during a victory. The role of the fans in the stands is to support, encourage, cheer, motivate and enjoy the fact that your child is able to compete in sports.

SOFTBALL STORY

I know that parents can get emotional and want the best for their child, not only in life, but also while competing in sports. All I'm asking is that the parent is careful with how they engage their child's coach. For example, I was coaching a 14-and-under girls' softball team. As I was giving instructions to one of my players who had been struggling with hitting, her parent shouted out from the stands, "Hey coach, don't mess with that. She's good with that. She has a professional hitting coach that I pay a lot of money for."

There is a time and a place for a parent to either challenge or question a coach's instruction or decision and, that time is not during an actual game while the coach is trying to coach and teach. The proper action would have been for the parent to approach the coach after the game and explain their concerns. If the concerns were that my coaching was conflicting with the professional training being received, then we should have had that discussion. If the parent had spoken to me after the game, I would have simply explained to the parent that their child showed me that she had just purchased a new bat, and it was my observation that the bat that was purchased was too heavy, and I noticed that she had a hard time getting around (bat speed was too slow), so I simply advised her to choke up on the bat in an effort to try to get her used to her new bat.

What we as parents don't realize, and I may have said this before in the book, you put a child in a peculiar situation when they have to take instruction from the coach and the parent. It causes a lot of confusion and adds to the pressure on the child while competing. You put a child in a situation where they have to not show respect to the coach because they don't want to disappoint the parent. You always have the option of selecting another team or coach, when the situation you're in is not a good fit for you and the child. Respect the fact that your child's coach is responsible for your child during practice and game time.

STAYING FOR YOUR CHILD'S PRACTICE

This is a concern of mine for multiple reasons. Let me start off with a situation that was brought to my attention during football season. Two football players were involved in a collision while participating in a drill at practice. They both suffered a concussion, and one of the players had to be transported to the hospital. My intent is not to blame anyone or point fingers, but just to show the importance of staying for your child's practice. I'm not sure of the child's age but I'm guessing he was an 8th grader. This player had to go to the hospital alone in the ambulance, but his parents did meet the ambulance at the hospital. I recall a parent stating that a coach should have ridden with the child to the hospital in the ambulance, which was a statement that I didn't agree with due to the fact that the majority of the coaches have their own children on the field to look after, get home for dinner and get homework done. I don't think it's fair to put that responsibility on a coach.

In this situation, I think a parent or guardian should have remained at the child's practice for the entire time. If you need to make a run, it should be quick and you should notify another parent as well as the coach that you are leaving and how long you're going to be. Also, provide your contact information to someone other than the coach to contact you in case of an emergency. For that reason alone, you should stay for your child's practice. Now, the other reason is for support, evaluation, and to obtain any information needed or being passed out. But mainly to make sure your child is treated properly and fairly. It also helps if you are there to check your child's behavior when needed.

NOT ENOUGH

It's game day and your son or daughter is excited. They are looking forward to connecting with their teammates to crack jokes, have some fun, get their snacks and get some points of encouragement from their fans and coaches. This is your child's focus, until they step out of the house, open the car door to get in and get settled, only to have mom or dad start the vehicle, and before all four of the tires on the vehicle complete a full rotation, the adult speaks. These are some of things that your child has to endure. The parent begins to speak and this is how it normally goes. Now, you know today is a big game. Don't forget what your coach told you. Hey when you get out there, no playing around. Be serious. How do you feel? If you're not going to take this serious, let me know now. All this has been said and you've only driven five minutes from the house.

So now that initial feeling your child had, when they were looking forward to their game, has diminished. The child initially was looking forward to going to his/her game. Without realizing it you the parent have already started taking the fun away before your child has gotten to the court or playing field. You've changed their mental focus. So now the child thinks once again my mom or dad is taking my sporting event to serious. Not realizing that this is supposed to be an outlet for the child and not another opportunity to discourage the child.

You finally arrive to your destination and your child sees all of the other children running, playing, laughing and having fun. The same situation they were thinking about before they left the house. The child finally gets a chance to be a child, then here comes the adult with more unwanted advice. Hey stop playing. Don't worry about your teammates, you need to go and stretch or go sit down. I don't think that parents realize that coaches teach during the week and children play during game time and that's when they get to show off all their hard work they put in and not all the high expectations the parents are trying to put on them. So now the game has started and your child is not doing too well and you're showing signs of being upset as if your child let you down. You're yelling things out to them out of frustration and now you're extra angry because your son or daughter doesn't seem to be paying you any attention.

You see, your child's day started out as a day that he or she was excited about, knowing they were going to be with their teammates and not whether they were going to win or lose, do well or do bad. All that was on their mind was having fun, and you ruined it with your adult logic, trying to put a certain mental advantage into your child's head. So now the game is coming to an end, and all the other children are taking the lost in stride, or should I say they are showing good sportsmanship, and they realize it's only a game and that youth sports are always to be fun. But your child has a look on his or her face as if they wanted to catch a cab home instead.

So now you're in the vehicle on your way home and it is quiet. The child knows the parent is upset with the events that occurred at the youth sporting event. Several minutes have passed, and then out of nowhere, "Where was your mind today?" If you didn't want to play today, you should have said something and I could have saved my gas and time. So now the child has a blank look on their face as if they can't believe that the same adult that states that just go out there and play hard and have fun, just totally changed. Here's my advice to you. If you are that parent, or have been that parent, try this approach. When preparing to take your child to his or her next game, just make sure they are prepared to participate. This means, make sure they have all of their equipment, tell them to have fun, do your best and you can ask them if they need a pep talk before their game.

On the way back home, if he or she didn't do well, just simply ask if they want to talk about it. If they say, no, then that's it. No further questions are needed. If they yes, just listen, and if you have to speak, only offer encouraging words. The purpose of this segment is to avoid the child from thinking that what he or she does is just not enough in the eyes of their parents.

WHO ARE YOU PUNISHING?

I challenge parents to think about the word "commitment," which is by definition the act of committing or pledging. Also it states that commitment is an obligation or promise. What jumps out at me the most is the word "obligation," followed by a promise. Here is the scenario. Your son or daughter is very important to their team's success. A situation arises. It may be something that happened in school or at home, and now you as the parent feel as though something has to take place to show your child that you are not pleased with their actions. In some cases, you've probably had this conversation before with your child about not doing whatever it is was that you were displeased with. So you decide to take the child off the team. While the team's season has taken a turn for the worst and it's due largely to the fact that your child is no longer a part of the team.

Now what? So was that out of convenience for you, since now you don't have to transport your child back and forth to practice and games? Or, you know that taking this child off the team would be devastating and that they will change their behavior immediately. Well, I can say this is the wrong answer. Because you see, even though you removed them from something to punish them, they somehow are still rewarded by your actions going forward. As soon as the initial anger or frustration has worn off, they're right back to watching TV, playing video games, eating out, purchasing the latest and greatest sneaker and the list goes on and on. And the word "commitment" has left the building.

Okay, let me stop right there and now give it a twist. You child's coach communicates with the parents and the child on a regular basis. He's always a phone call away. He prays with your child. He visits your child's school. He randomly checks on your child and provides a positive environment during practices and games. I ask you, who are you punishing? What message are you really sending? The message is, it's an inconvenience for you.

In the beginning of the chapter, I referred to a child that was an important factor to his or her team. In reality, all of the children that participate are important because at the end of the day your teaching commitment is a must-have character trait in life. Once again, my motto is PASS which stands for Prayer-Academics-Structure-Success.

If all coaches, parents and children follow these simple steps, everyone would benefit from the results. Removing a child off a structured system is the wrong thing to do. You see every little bit helps. The majority of our children struggle and make bad decisions at some point in their lives. Sometimes this is a result of a lack of structure, and as parents we have to sit down with our children and come up with recovery methods other than punishing methods. Punishing methods should be a thing of the past. Children today prepare themselves for punishment because they know what to expect and we as parents don't come up with creative ways to teach discipline to our children.

I encourage you to take time out with your child and figure out recovery methods, which is simply something a child can fall back on when he or she falls. It can be a scripture from the bible or a movie that has touched you in a particular way. The thing that I find that works the best is for the parents to sit down and come up with their own words of wisdom or a self-check list for the child. Removing a child from a team is not punishment. It's giving them more freedom and idle time to do something that's counter-productive. This will take them back to the same cycle of wrong doing and losing focus. I close with this, children get in trouble because they lose their focus and without recovery and focus, there is failure.

PUNISHMENT

I'm not saying that a child should be taken off a team, but we need to consider what the child has done and measure your actions based on the incident. Now, if it's something that's a criminal offense, or if the child is fighting or involved with drugs, or even using profanity, then the problem is larger than we think. I do think we should have the child come to his or her practice and talk to their teammates and give their teammates an apology. Explain their action and have them give their teammates a resolution, and at that point either the child, the parent, coach or one of the child's teammates should come together and pray. This process brings awareness to other children that may prevent them from making the same mistakes. Many children want to get this right away but with anything that's good, there is always a process before you receive the final product or results.

This is simply called accountability, which helps with the mental growth of any child that is able, and willing to speak to their peers, even the child that has a problem speaking out. Have them write a letter to their teammates. Also, if you know that your son or daughter has behavior problems, whether it's at school or home, notify your coach at the start of the season and put them on point that throughout the course of the season my child may not attend all practices or games because of their past experiences. At the start of my seasons, I let my parents know that if your child for whatever reason can't attend practice due to anything dealing with family or school he or she will not penalized. I will always understand and assure them that their child will not be penalized for it on game day.

I look at it this way, you come to practice to learn and prepare for whatever sport you're participating in. So why should I punish or penalize you for staying home to learn or prepare for what you need to do in school, that day or that night, that week or even in some cases, that month.

I refuse to put sports before your child's growth at home or in school. I'm not going to give a child double punishment by not allowing them to participate on game day when I know that putting the effort into what they're doing is required of them. Some coaches may say well, the child missed a lot or we put a lot of stuff in. Well if he or she is a good youth sports coach, then they should be able to figure out a way to get your child involved and place them in a situation where they can succeed. Let's reward the child for handling their responsibility. And the final decision should be the parents and not the coach, and that's just how I look at it. Some coaches may differ.

So in conclusion, we need to realize why we are removing the child from the team, and in most cases removing the child is not a good idea even though it may hurt them. That hurt is only going to last for a little while. It's not going to affect them long-term. The people that will suffer the most may be his or her teammates. So let's also consider everyone that is involved.

Change is Not Always Good

In competitive basketball, certain children go from team to team, and that is what is messing up youth competitive basketball. Parents will quit a team and go to another team and expect different results. But it is the same parent, same child and same skill level, which you are bringing to the new team, if the parent or athlete don't recognize there faults, then moving to a different team is not going to solve the problem. You may take your child to a team that is successful and is winning, and often time the coach will focus more of his attention on plays, schemes and sets and ways to win a basketball game instead of the overall growth of the student athlete on and off the court.

These children will come to my team and expect to play right away, when they were on their previous team or teams, they were getting minimum playing time, but want to come to my team and get a lot of playing time. I tell parents that winning is not my first focus. I teach them how to win and to lose. I have had children that come to my team that have parents that are out of control that thinks their child is great. If they were as good as their parents claim they are, they would dominate, and take advantage of all their opportunities, but they don't because of their mindset and behavioral problems. I have had parents who ignore the behavior of a child that does poorly in school, and has no respect for others. Since he's an outstanding basketball player with a possible future in basketball on the next level, they expect me to ignore his off the court behavior as well. They expect me to allow the child to join my team and to play, while I ignore his disruptive behavioral patterns on and off the court. Parents point these problems out to me, sometimes in advance but often times, I find out over time. When I am confronted with laziness, personal desires to quit and overall bad attitudes from certain athletes; I expect the parents to recognize that they play a very important role in defusing this type of behavior at home and prior to the child coming to practice or a game.

I hear parents yelling, "Shoot the ball" not realizing the play was for him to not shoot. Who do you think the child will listen to? The parent is putting even more pressure on the child to listen to them and disrespect the coach. You as a parent are giving your child another dosage of do what you want to do because now the child is not listening to the coach and the parent is disrupting what we are trying to accomplish as a team. It is not their fault because the parents are putting the pressure on them and making them think they are great at such a young age. They blow up on the child if they lose, and they curse at them if they are not doing well. That is just wrong. These children would not do well.

I can coach them but not play the game for them. After and during the game, the parent's face is angry at the child and that forces them to shut down. It feeds negative energy into the child that will stick with them for the rest of their lives. It stays in and builds up in their child's mind. We were playing games and the games that we should win but were not pulling them out. The parents were yelling instructions, whether bad or good, fussing and cursing and just loud. As soon as the child makes a mistake, you fuss at them as a parent. Then for me as the coach, I need to coach and also reel your child back in. As the season went on, parents wanted to pull them from my team and put them on another team. Coaches would be willing to take the children, and now you have taught the child not to keep a commitment. Always go somewhere where you can win. They don't learn about the concept of character building, leadership, or commitment. You allow them to go from team to team. You are up in the stands watching your child lose and get upset. But when the game is over, the child is fine until the adult brings it back up. The child is fine. At the end of the day, all it is an organized activity for your child to participate in to clear their mind from their studies.

Stop putting in the child's heads that they have to do this to get scholarships because you don't have money to send them to college. What kind of message is that? Americans have their children thinking that they have to excel in sports in order to go to college. That is too much pressure on a youth athlete. I mean eighth graders on down. But it affects all children. When children go to high school and college, the coaches are coaching to keep their jobs, so you do not know what you are going to get from a high school or college coach in terms of how they instruct your child because they are coaching to maintain their jobs, which is a lot different from a volunteer coach. We don't get paid anything.

We give up our time and energy for your child, dealing with their shortcomings, behavioral problems, and skill sets. I had children that had jump shots and no defense, or could play defense but not score, but the children would not see that. The parents would just want their child to shine without thinking about anyone else on the team. These children were excited about my attending the schools. I got their grades up. They would turn their homework in and they would do their reading logs. I would go in and motivate them and get them do what they want to do. I do this on my own, voluntarily. I had to remove a couple of these children and do something different because I wanted to trigger something in their minds to go about their athletics and academics differently. The children tried to go to better teams and they end up on those teams' benches. On my team, at least they were enjoying the game of basketball. The parents would put the child in this negative situation that would disrupt his performance.

I had a real tall child whose basketball skill level was low. He was a good, sweet child that didn't really want to be a player and never really progressed. He seemed to have been pushed by the parents. The basketball community saw a big child and recruited him off of my team and the child ultimately did not have the skill set and did not get a lot of playing time while on my team. It was my opinion at the time that the young man really didn't have the same desire for his self as others had for him.

In those type of situation the mentoring side of me comes out, and that's to make sure I'm not doing anything to the athlete, that will cause any type of embarrassment or discouragement to the child, my point is that a coach has to be patient with certain players even if the parent thinks otherwise. As a parent, I recommend that you have constant dialogue with your coach and child to make sure that your child is having some form of growth, and find out what's your child's coach expectation is for your child.

Chapter 3

THE COACH

Coach by definition is an instructor, which to me is very general. My definition of the word "coach" is as follows: a coach is someone that provides structure, discipline, guidance, integrity, mentoring, counseling and a foundation. My definition of a "youth coach" is someone that provides support, stresses the importance of education, stresses the importance of prayer, setting goals, building character, creating leaders, teaching youth athletes how to lose with dignity and with respect by respecting your opponents. Of course, I can go on for a while, but I figure you get where I'm going with this.

My message to all coaches is that we have a God-given duty to give all of God's children that we have the opportunity to coach, or the ones that we have coached, the best preparation for life that we can offer, and not just our knowledge to win a sporting event since our youth gravitate to our every word and every action. Let's please be careful with our approach to coaching our youth on and off the playing field. All of a child's behavior is learned behavior. So please let's be mindful of the things we are teaching either directly or indirectly because the athletes are always watching, literally.

History shows that the majority of youth coaches both male and female started coaching because of their child. That can be good or bad for the child and the team. Good if you get a parent that is fair and firm, but bad if the coach's intent is to only cater to their child. I will revisit coaching your own child later. The role of a head coach in youth sports is huge. You see, as the head coach, you have to make sure everything is right from your assistant coaches to your team administration. You have to have a vision, a mission, patience and tolerance. There are many styles and approaches to coaching, but in youth sports everyone should be close as it relates to coaching methods. I've come up with a standard we all should duplicate, and that is coaches should incorporate P.A.S.S., which simply stands for Prayer, Academics, Structure and Success.

We need to explain to our student athlete that going to school is the easiest part of life. The hardest part comes when they become adults. Of course, they're going to always have something going on that will require them to come up with solutions on their own, and without a good education, they're not going to have a good and productive life. And for the rest of their lives, they will be tested in all aspects and every day in their lives.

Let's stop focusing all of our attention on the athletes that can help your teams win games and start focusing the majority of your attention on those athletes that you think will hurt your chances of winning the game. We, as coaches, should be geared to making sure all of our players receive more than adequate instructions. I may have said this several times in this book, but our actions as coaches affect children more than just during a youth sporting event. We, as coaches, are really becoming the front line of defense for our youth athletes, each day, each practice, each game and each year. The clock is ticking.

What will be your purpose for coaching? We know the world is changing and opportunities are disappearing for those that are not adequately prepared. We, as human beings, lose every day, but that's not our focus when we are coaching; however, it's a big part of life. We wonder why our children lose focus, drop out of school, and resort to bullying, doing drugs, committing crimes, and being disrespectful. This is due to the fact that we, as adults, promote win, win, and win.

And when our children lose, they are stuck and the resolution they seek is to go gain respect by doing all of these negative things because in the eyes of their peers, being tough and popular at all cost is considered a victory. So what's my point? Use coaching as a vehicle to reach and save our children, since we have their undivided attention and teach them how to recover from a lose. Try getting to the root of losing and maybe we will start seeing a balance in our children's lives. I've seen coaches bend over backwards for athletes that exhibit superior talent by bending the rules, pushing the envelope, overlooking things like deadlines for registration and parents that aren't very cooperative, but they had to have those children. Then, on the other hand, if the children weren't game changers, there wouldn't be any sense of urgency on pushing back deadlines or putting up with disgruntled parents. Coaches remember all eyes are on you. You're not just teaching the children, you are also teaching other coaches, parents and by-standers.

As coaches, we should want people to say, "Now that's a coach that gets it." That statement simply means you're the caliber of coach that understands your role and your purpose. And not your winning percentage for games but your winning percentage for changing lives, which brings me to the recognition portion of the book. These gentlemen at some point coached my sons, or I have witnessed their coaching styles over the years. On behalf of the children, parents and myself, I would like to say <u>Thank You</u>, for being youth coach pioneers.

God got it right when he touched these hearts and lead them to coach. At this time I would like to recognize, Coach Rick Taylor who is the President of Patuxent Rhinos, Coach Guy Queen, Coach Malcolm Drewery, Coach Keith Rogers, Coach Preston Boyd, Coach Derek Smith, Coach Kevin Washington, Coach Bert Watson, Coach Darryl Haraway, Coach Ty, Coach Mark Woods, Coach Reggie Washington, Coach Anthony Whitehead, Coach Moe Williams, Coach Derian Quick, Coach Bertille Roc Bridgeman, Coach Daryl Foote, Coach Keith Morris, Coach Stink, Coach Tim Taylor, Coach

Moshe Imel, Coach Mark Landon, Coach Abraham, Coach Al Watson, Coach Brian Thompson, Coach Reginald Powell, Coach Chane Clingman, Coach David Pope, Coach Marina Akers-Epps, Coach Cheryl Rothwell, Coach Shemia Anderson, Coach Tyrone Massenburg and the Greenwood Brothers Donald and Ronald, two dynamite brothers that go beyond the norm to reach our youth athletes. May God continue to bless each and every one of you. If we're not teaching, then we're not reaching. So coaches let's mentor our children to ensure that they reach their true potential, whether in an athletic environment or educational setting. Let's ensure that the individual thrives and increases his or her level of self-confidence.

Assistant Coaches

Assistant coaches, there are a lot of things with assistant coaches that I've learned over the years. I know it's tough being an assistant coach, especially when you have the insight and ideas of your own. What you need to do is make sure you're on the same page with your head coach and make sure he gives you an idea of what your role is and find out how much input you have. There are times for whatever reason that the assistant coach slanders the head coach by saying negative things to the parents and players, I guess, in an attempt to win them over.

What assistant coaches fail to realize is that if the head coach didn't see something in you that he felt was in line with the mentoring and teaching that he plans on giving to the children, he would not have put you on his staff. This is the reason why you should respect the head coach. Give him as much respect as he gave you, when he put you on his staff. Give him your full support on decision-making and be willing to offer advice when you think it's necessary.

 I had a situation one year, and the reason why I wanted to share this with you is to show cause and effect. One day, I couldn't attend practice, and I left word for my assistant coaches to work on one play because I had plans on using this play in the upcoming game. So to practice this play would have taken about 15 minutes to go over, and then the assistant coaches would have had the remainder of the practice to implement whatever they like. It's game day and the game is really competitive, score is close, may even be tied up.

I turn to one of my assistant coaches and asked, "Hey did you guys get that play in?" and he told me no, but we added something else. Now put yourself in my shoes. How would you have felt? Not only did they not work on my play, but also they implemented their own play. So how should I take this? All I asked was that one play be worked on for a few minutes. I like to consider myself a coach that doesn't run a dictatorship, but one that allows his staff to have styles of coaching and their own thought processes.

How do the assistant coaches betray the head coaches without thinking about how they actually became assistant coaches? The head coach had to see something in them to put them on the staff. If the head coach saw something in you, they shouldn't be penalized. I always like to put coaches on my staff that have been head coaches somewhere else. I want to put the best possible people in place so that my children can learn from them, not because they are someone's fathers. I want quality people on my staff.

I have had coaches on my staff that would talk behind my back and talk to the parents and say a whole bunch of negative things. Those particular coaches do not teach or instruct, but come game time, their only concern is how their child is doing. Many get on the staff to coach their children, not the entire team. That is a major problem.

At the youth level you just show an interest or let the president of the organization know you have an interest, and you can get credentialed. Prince Georges County has a test to be a coach. I've taken several tests through the years. They do background checks.

On several occasions, I have had to remove a coach from my coaching staff. They either showed too much anger, did not mirror my method of coaching, used profanity, showed a lot of favoritism to their children or betrayed my trust, as far as helping the children that we are coaching.

INEXPERIENCED COACHES

Now we come to the inexperienced coaches. Inexperience is not always based on how long you've been coaching, but to me it's based on your experience with coaching youth athletics. You must know how to deal with children. Coaching requires patience, which is a very important trait that is needed to coach youths. You may be able to win a lot, and your philosophy may be intact, but you must be experienced as a mentor or role model. These two are critical. As mentors you teach life skills and demonstrate life skills as a role model. An inexperienced coach can be stubborn. He doesn't want to learn. They think they just got it. As a youth coach you must listen and learn all the time. Then you have those coaches that coach their children. I remember one season when I was coaching basketball, a parent said, "Man, you're the head coach. Your son should never come off the court." I told that dad that I would always coach my sons just like anyone else on my team. Meaning, my sons aren't going to get any special treatment.

Through the years, I would be asked if I have a child on the team because the way I conduct myself you would never know if my sons played for me. I take that as a compliment, but you do have a lot of coaches that got into coaching just to coach their own child. And their main focus is their child. Now, some may say that that is wrong, and then you, on the other hand, have people that think it's cool. I do know that as a coach you should cater to your entire team, from your strongest child to your weakest child. We, as coaches, have to teach integrity. We have to teach sportsmanship. We have to provide guidance. We have to make ourselves available for our youth athletes 24/7. There are going to be parents in your ear telling you that you're doing great and those that think you're horrible, especially the ones that talk behind your back. With all this going on, you still have to keep your focus. Meaning, you have to stay true to your vision and purpose.

Let me give you a couple of scenarios. My son is playing in high school. This is a basketball scenario on how some high school basketball coaches approach the game. The team is losing by 40 points in a game that is late in the third period. The talent on the opposing team was far better than the talent my son's team had. Everyone in attendance knew that it would be impossible for our team to come back. Being a parent, I'm upset because I'm trying to figure out why my son, along with several other players that don't get a lot of playing time, are not being put in the game and the team is losing by 40 points.

This is me reacting as a parent and as a coach. I'm not only talking about my child but there were other children who also make the sacrifice to play a high school sport and maintain their grades, that work hard at practice every day, and we are talking about a junior varsity team that doesn't have playoff games or a championship. In my experience, this means that the JV team should be a developmental team that should prepare the young men for varsity for the following season. So now I'm in the stands and the clock is winding down and there is no sign of my son getting in.

So I get upset and come from the bleachers so I can position myself to get the coach's attention so I can greet him as he is walking off the court. So, you tell me as a parent; was that right or was that wrong? As a parent, I thought it was the right thing to do since I was defending my child based on ethics. But as a coach, after I did it, I thought to myself, how I would have felt if a parent came to me talking about his or her child's playing time. Most coaches would be offended. When I approached the coach, I said the team was losing, and there was no way we could win the game. "Are you trying to tell me you couldn't allow my son some playing time based on the game?" The coach's response was, "You know, dad, this isn't boys and girls club basketball." I told him, "Don't insult my intelligence because I'm a coach as well. I've been coaching for years. The principle of this is you guys don't have playoffs, and you don't have a championship. This is strictly developmental. What happened was you were losing by 40 points and you got into your feelings and lost focus as a coach.

You weren't even thinking about putting the other children in. You were only thinking that you were losing badly, and you couldn't recover or pull out this game, meaning you knew you didn't have a chance to win. That caused you to forget about everyone else that was affected by your decision and the value of the situation. In defeat there are also ways to teach by building on a negative and allow others to gain experience. What's the difference in winning by 40 points and making sure everyone plays and losing by 40 points and making sure everyone plays? There is none. You will lose, you may win, but as long as you work hard and help others along the way your rewards will come. So never stop pursuing your goals."

So my advice to all coaches is, no matter what you're coaching, be mindful of all your actions and all your players no matter what level you're coaching on. These athletes are still human beings that possess feelings, so to my high school coaches and above, don't be so quick to come across as if boys and girls club athletics don't matter because we all know for most athletes that's where it all starts, and that there are many coaches in that arena that are volunteering valuable time. So as coaches on all levels, let's be fair to all of our athletes, since we are dealing with children' lives, their growth, their mindsets and their futures.

Another scenario that deals with one of my sons is regarding baseball. I like to start my scenario off by saying by no means is this a shot at a coach or the school program, but it is my attempt to bring awareness to what I believe to be a negative situation in the eyes of the athletes and their parents. So, you tell me how you would feel.

My son received MVP honors both freshmen and sophomore years while playing junior varsity baseball. Mind you, the varsity coach told me that my child was unable to play varsity baseball because of his size, even though he had the skills to compete with the players that were currently on the team.   As long as you are coaching, don't ever tell a child or parent that they can't play baseball or any other sport based on their size and stature.

If they have the talent, then it's up to you as a coach to put them in a situation where they can't get hurt. So now my child is a junior, and mind you, he played junior varsity his freshman and sopho-more year. He carried the team. He was like the rock of the team. He pitched and played shortstop. Second, he was the best hitter on the team, so now he is on varsity.

So now, my son is practicing. He is starting in all of the games leading up to the first regular season game.   In the first game of the season, the coach decides to start a freshman in front of my child. We're talking about a ninth grader that hasn't paid any dues in the high school program. When I was in high school, in order for a freshman to make a varsity team, his skill set had to be outstanding. Back in those days, coaches respected the seniority of the seniors and juniors and their hard work over the years in the program; basically, you had to wait your turn.   Remember, my son was MVP two years straight, and the coach had a freshman playing in front of a junior who had already established himself in the program and who had aspirations to further his baseball career after high school.

I believe that coaches should sit down with their athletes on an individual basis and discuss with them their goals and aspirations regarding the sport. Is that fair? Also, when you looked around, you saw the child in question or even all of the other children and you noticed, those parents stay in the coach's ear. That's another thing to coaches, stop allowing parents to persuade you one way or another. Show some integrity and be fair to all of those children that work hard.

Don't play a child because the dad was a former coach somewhere else, the parent is a friend, they're bringing Gatorade, keeping the score book, or doing things to get on your good side just so their child can play when you know their skill level is not comparable to the junior and seniors that you already have on the team. Keep it fair.

So I approached the coach. Like with anything, I respect head coaches, and unless the situation merits me talking to the head coach, I won't approach the head coach. But I had to because it was bothering me and it was bothering my son. Shortly after that, things seem to turn around. He started playing the children that should play as opposed to the children whose parents were pressuring him to play them.

Playing Time

I want to start out by giving a couple of scenarios based on actual youth sporting events. It was a beautiful fall day in September, which means football season is upon us. The student athletes had been preparing for this day since the beginning of July, they had endured not only hot workouts, but also the demands of both their coaches and parents that they do their best and are at their best by the time the season began. So, as we all know, there are several different types of football players and we are talking about youth football players 8 – 14. You have the child that loves football, the child that is participating because he's being forced, the child that just wants to be with his friends, the child that needs to be a part of something that's constructive to keep him out of trouble and the child that just doesn't want to be there. This is the child that just doesn't know what he wants to do. He's out there, and it shows that he doesn't want to be out there and maybe he just doesn't want to let anyone down, he also knows that someone in his family is excited about him even making an effort to participate in something positive.

I know of a young man who, even though he wasn't the best football player, had given all he had during the days leading up to the first game of the season. You see, the previous school year, this young man would get bad grades, get suspended and the list goes on and on, but towards the end of the school year, things started to turn around for him. He had to attend summer school where he did great, finishing with two A's and two B's. And in order for him to play football in the fall, he had to do well in summer school, and that he did. So he was awarded the chance to play football, and during the months before the start of the season his playing ability never reached the standards of this one particular coach, who was obsessed with winning.

So moving forward, the parents and relatives, friends and etc. would often ask the young man when his season would start because they wanted to come and support him, and he would always say that he didn't know, but what he really wanted to say was that his coach was a jerk and his only interest was winning with the better children on his team.

So, this is the point I'm getting at, all coaches need to be mindful of all their players' aspirations and their pasts while the student athletes are under his watch because our actions as coaches affect a lot, not just on the field of play, but more so after the last whistle has blown.

Continuing the story, it was a beautiful fall day in September and it's the first game of the season. The young man's parents have invited several people to come out to support their son, since over the summer he has shown great signs of wanting to change his life and to better himself. At the game as people are walking from their cars to the field, you can see smiles and hear good conversations. We all know that those smiles represent proud parents, grandparents, relatives, friends and youth football fans. Because you see, the mere fact that these young men are a part of something positive is a plus. Now the game has started and the first quarter has ended and he hasn't gotten in yet. Now, its half time, and he hasn't gotten in yet. The end of the 3rd quarter is upon us and he hasn't gotten in. What a lot of coaches fail to realize is that this is a problem, and the cause and effect on this young man and others can plague them for the rest of their lives. We are now in the 4th and last quarter of the game with two minutes remaining. I'm not sure of the score, because in youth sports, that doesn't matter to me due to the fact that all youth sports is supposed to be developmental for all children that participate. So now, the game has ended and this child never touched the field.

Let's go back to the beginning for a second. We are talking about a young man that didn't do well in school, stayed in trouble, but decided to turn his life around, did great in summer school, gave his best during practice all the way up to the beginning of the season, had his parents, grandparents, relatives and friends at his game, and you mean to tell me that this coach or his coaching staff couldn't find a situation to put this child in the game? After all he's been through, to me this is not what youth sports are supposed to represent. This goes on all over the country and it's done in youth male sports as well as youth women sports. This brings me to a point that oftentimes people debate with me about and that's playing time on the high school level.

This is what I often hear from high school coaches. Well moms and dads, this is not boys and girls club anymore; this is high school, and when I hear that, all I say is blah, blah, blah to myself. You see, high school is an extension to boys and girls club sports, so let me explain. I totally understand that in high school, it is all about winning state championships, etc., and guess what, the only teams that get recognized for winning a state championship are those athletes that are playing varsity sports, not freshman teams and not JV teams. So let me get to my point. If you're a freshman coach, develop all your players--and you do this during practice days and game days--so that all of the student athletes that you selected for the season have a chance to compete and have a fair shot to make

JV or in some special cases to even make varsity, but that's stretching it. Because you see it's also a waste of time to have a 10th grader on varsity watching instead of playing.

To all my freshman coaches, I get it, you may someday aspire to be the JV coach with your final goal being the varsity coach, but my advice to you is just don't do it at the expense of our student athletes. For example, your primary goal shouldn't be to go undefeated. As a matter of fact, your goal should be to get your entire freshman team strong. I see it all the time, the starters make the same mistakes as the guys coming off the bench, and in many cases, they make more mistakes because they get more playing time. When the student athlete comes off the bench, his mistake is magnified like it's the end of the world and he's committed a major crime. Freshman coaches should think about entire team and not self-promotion. No one talks about an undefeated freshman team, 5, 10, 15 or 20 years down the road.

To my JV coaches, I understand your position. There are two different JV situations, one being your high school having freshman sports, which means 9th graders only, and then you have high schools that don't have freshman sports. To my JV coaches without freshman sports, understand staying power means, you have to produce wins in order for the varsity coach or the school to retain you for the following season. Here's my advice when having to talk with the varsity coach during the off-season. Find out from him what his expectations are for the team's growth and your growth, because if he or she doesn't have any expectation for your growth, then you really need to put your players first and that means all of them. If he tells you that when he's gone he wants you to take over, then good for you, but don't bank on that happening cause you best believe if the varsity coach is not doing well, and you have the JV job because of him, well rest assured you will be out of there, too. But let me not get off track cause this chapter is not about adults; it's about fair and equal play for our student athletes.

So JV coaches, find out your Head Varsity Coach's vision, and then explain your vision to him. And please allow me to put these words or thoughts in your head, and that is you want to assure him that first of all you're going to produce quality athletes for the following season and by doing this you may not go undefeated, and you may not win most of your games, but what you will be successful in doing is making your JV program stronger by giving all those players confidence and the desire to compete for a Varsity roster spot. JV coaches do it for the student athletes and not self-pride.

To my Varsity coaches, you are up. I totally get that on your level it's all about winning and getting those student athletes to the next level, such as getting them to college, creating leaders, creating fine young men and young women to be promising citizens in our communities, and I applaud all of you. I ask one favor, encourage your freshman coaches, if your school has freshman athletics and have them to develop all of the student athletes and give all the players playing time. And if you know the student athlete doesn't have what it takes, male or female, then have that conversation with the individual and his or her parents. Let's get out of this avoiding parent confrontations mode.

Often times, if you put everything on the table, you won't have any issues, cause they will have all the info, and please just give the facts. Also Varsity coaches, encourage your JV coaches to create some diamonds-in-the-ruff players. Like I said in early chapters, if you have 30 athletes on your team, that means you're dealing with 30 different expectations, and your job as a coach is to connect with all the players and see what they need to be their best and not what we coaches think what they need. Talk to the mother, the father, brothers, sisters, grandparents, etc. to see what advice you can get about their family member cause they know a whole lot more about the student athlete than you, especially on how and what motivates the student athlete. My final thoughts on this chapter (Playing Time) is to not play a student athlete will have more effect on his or her life than the effect it will have on your program, especially if the student athlete is not aware or doesn't have a clear understanding of their role or their coach's expectations. From youth sports to JV, coaches play all your children, every game. There shouldn't be a game that a student athlete shouldn't take part in, whether there is a mandatory play rule or not.

COMMENTS FROM OUR STUDENT ATHLETES ABOUT PLAYING TIME, MALE AND FEMALE, AGES 8-17

1. Not playing a lot because of height and size, felt bad cause I didn't get a chance to show what I could do.
2. Participated in practice every day, worked hard, kept my grades up, was reliable. That still wasn't enough.
3. Didn't get much playing time until last home game.
4. Didn't really want to go to the game, but didn't want to be a quitter.
5. I wanted my family to come but didn't want them to waste their time and money.
6. Coaches feed off of a couple of players and no backups when the star players were hurt because they didn't work with anyone else. The reserves lacked confidence.
7. Should work all players during practice so they can be used during different situations.
8. Star players could get away with coming to practice late or sometimes not coming at all and still start.
9. Coaches set rules and standards, but don't follow them.
10. Work ethic and skill should dictate playing time.
11. Working hard at practice and receiving no playtime makes you feel like you're working for nothing.
12. Coaches punish you for bringing things to their attention when you're trying to be treated fairly.
13. It's not right when you tell some players they couldn't play because they had been sick but other players could be disrespectful to the coaches and still get to play.

14. When people ask me why I'm not playing, I didn't have a reason to give them, so I would say ask the coach, cause I really don't know why.
15. Coach doesn't trust the other players enough to put them in the game for fear of mistakes, but the children on the court are making mistake after mistake.

These are words from our student athletes. I could actually write a separate book on playing time and how it affects student athletes, parents and coaches.

SHAKE IT OFF

In a lot of sports, especially if it involves your key players, a lot of coaches try to impose their own type of remedy or therapy. They will try to assist without real technical or medical experience instead of seeing what the real problem is, and they do not know what they are talking about. A lot of times they just say, "Shake it off," trying to heal the child before the child can speak for himself. Last year, a child came and complained about his wrist and said it was really bad. The assistant coach opens his hand, and tells the child to punch his hand as hard as he could. I couldn't believe my eyes. We later learned that the child had a fractured wrist. By him telling him to punch his hand, the coach could have made it worse than it was.

What I do if one of the children get injured is tell them to relax, and have them explain what's hurting, and I allow the player to take as long as they need to get themselves together. I have seen children get carted off the field, and often it takes a while for the medical unit to respond. Organizations should figure out a way to make sure there's always a medical unit on the scene for the entire time games are being played, or identify someone in your organization that has medical experience. They seldom have them at high school games. Football is a contact sport and it is a matter of minutes within which you need to respond, instead of people guessing what the issue or problem is. Can you feel my hand? Can you wiggle your toes? If the child says "no," then they ask the questions that they know they can get a certain "yes" from.

Nine times out of ten, they get a "yes." If the child says something opposite, then they panic. Someone should have been onsite. You have firefighters and police officers. Why not put those people on point? Have them bring their first aid bag and just be ready. Youth athletic programs should have medics and security. There should be a whole host of people volunteering, not just coaches.

REFEREES

This area of youth sports is so overlooked it's crazy. I hope you will understand and have a different perspective when I'm done. This is for coaches, parents and our youth athletes. First off, referees should be treated with the utmost respect, and everyone should know that on all levels of competition, no matter the sport. A referee, umpire, field judge has the job or task to ensure that there is fair play at all times. My first paragraph should be something that should be articulated to all athletes before their perspective seasons start, so allow me to give you my understanding of the position of the referees or any other person who is responsible for safe and fair play.

Referees are an extension of youth coaches. As a matter of fact, all coaches. What I do before any contest is first introduce myself to the game referees and then I begin to explain my purpose and what I expect from them. That is, simply for the referees to teach my players the rules of the game by making the best calls they can make and to show my athletes professionalism. I pride myself on not debating with referees or getting frustrated with them. I'm totally aware that we all make mistakes.

It's not fair to the referees for us, as coaches, parents or athletes to badger a referee's judgment on his or her calls. Besides, we all know that on the youth and high school levels the referees don't have the luxury of going over to a monitor or replay booth like they have in college and professional sports. This should tell us that they understand human error exists and don't want a bad call to be a determining factor in a game. To recap, I'm basically saying please monitor your behavior as coaches and parents because our athletes are listening and watching your actions. Since all behavior is learned behavior, when our youth are involved, please take note.

AFTER A LOSS CONVERSATION

The majority of our youth student athletes aren't mature enough or don't have enough life experiences as it relates to losing, during a competitive sporting event, or the final result that ends in a loss. That's because often the emphasis is put on winning, and not enough time is put on how to lose with class. I can recall talking to one of my football players after a loss. I must take my hat off to this young man (Malik Bridgeman). A couple of seasons ago, this young man would just lose it, but as he matured he realized that youth sports is to simply develop you and get you prepared to play high school sports.

So I said to Malik, "Think about this, both teams compete to win, and if for some reason, you are on the losing end, you should acknowledge the winning players with a sincere congratulation and say things to them like, 'Good win. I enjoyed the competition. You guys were the better team today, etc." What will happen is that the other team will also realize that, not only are you a good athlete, but a good person with great character, and you can believe that the next time you see the team again, not only are they going to remember how good an athlete you are, they are going to always respect you when they see you on or off the field of play. I also explained to Malik that in every lost, there's a victory to the losing team as well. For instance, when you lose, this should motivate you to work hard, take practice serious, and respect your coaches and the time they volunteer. There is victory also in a loss as you mature and grow, and think about someone's parent, grandparent, brother, sister, friend etc., may have been going thru something in their life, and at that moment of a victory, the winning team puts a smile on someone's face that turns into a lifetime memory.

So I'm writing this chapter because I think that this is one of the most important aspects in youth sports and in life. The fact is that we have lost more in life then we win. The overall victory is life and being alive. People go to funerals and celebrate life with songs, prayers, memories etc., but after a loss, the demeanor is somber and sad. Why? I know I may have stated this somewhere else in this book, but this is important. Which leads me into this; I recall losing a spring football game. The spring football season is something we call in the GMYFL Greater Metropolitan Youth Football League, which is a five-week challenge with a championship showcase at the end of the spring season.

So, mind you, the spring season is just something to get the young men some time to work on some skills and fundamentals, and it's like a warm-up for the upcoming fall season. My team made it to the championship game on Sunday following an emotional high-energy victory over one of our league's powerhouse teams, the Baltimore Stallions, which is an outstanding youth organization based out of Baltimore MD. After that victory, my team had the opportunity the following day to face the team that we loss to in the first game of the spring season, the Maryland Seahawks. The game was a highly anticipated rematch. Without going into a lot of details about the game, I will at least say that there were several momentum shifts in the game, and when it was all said and done, my team wound up on the losing end.

Here's the substance of this chapter. You see when a coach is winning he's the best, but when a coach loses, people find fault. I get the whole point of this is how people are, etc., but in youth sports, there's no place for this kind of behavior. Let me explain why. You see, a coach like myself puts more time in off the field with my student athletes than I do on the field. I do school visits on Mondays and Tuesdays, and I do student athletes and parent consultations on the weekends, and all of this is free of charge. So, I would like to encourage the adults that openly express the dislike in the play calling, personnel and everything else that takes place during a youth sporting event, to be mindful of the damage you can do to the player/ coach relationship.

Telling your son or daughter your coach is a bad coach, and that the coach doesn't know what he's doing is wrong. Forgetting about all those extra hours of educating, life skills, character building and everything else we coaches do to create well-rounded student athletes. You can destroy all that progress by saying one negative comment to your child about his or her coach, and at the end of the day is it that serious, to be so negative towards a coach. Also, after a loss, the only comments that should be coming out of an adult's mouth is all of the positive things that came out of the youth sporting event, cause children often react a certain way because they are anticipating what their moms or dads are going to say negative about the game.

Let's all try and find a positive in a loss because there are many lessons to be learned in a loss. In closing, consistently support your coach through the good and the bad, cause not only are coaches dealing with multiple personalities, including parents, during the season, they definitely don't need any extra distractions, especially when you know your child is a handful off the field. Teach your child that a loss is not a bad thing, and let them know if you play sports, you are going to lose.

Chapter 4

THE LADY EAGLES OF EXCELLENCE CHRISTIAN SCHOOL

My favorite coaching story ironically isn't about any of my sons. One of the schools my sons attended was seeking coaches for the elementary and middle school basketball teams. I told the athletic director I would be interested in whichever team was left without a coach. The athletic director called me back and asked me if I would have a problem coaching girls. Without hesitation, I told her that would not be a problem. When I got off of the phone, I realized what I had just gotten myself into. I have three sons. I have never coached girls in anything. Now, I had the task of coaching 4th, 5th and 6th grade girls.

My first day of practice was incredibly funny. I was clueless on how my first day was going to play out. As the girls trickled into the gym, my first thought was I need an assistant, preferably a female assistant. I reached out to Mrs. Anderson. She wasn't sure if she had the time to assist me, but I asked her to just consider it. I'm walking back into the gym and I don't hear balls bouncing, no yelling, screaming--nothing. The gym is empty. I go back into Mrs. Anderson's office and I asked, "Where did the girls go?"

She said, "Oh, they went to get snacks." Snacks, are you serious! She said, yes snacks. She patted me on my back and said, "Good luck, Coach." Now the last time someone said those words to me, I had a lot of work ahead of me. With a whistle in my mouth, standing at half court with my arms folded (tough guy right), they started slowly coming back into the gym, paying me no attention. Finally, two girls approached me, Diamond and Mariah, and simply said, "Hi Coach." I said, "Hello." I said, "So when can I start practice?"

Diamond puts her finger to her temple and says, "Hmmm, let me think." Then another young lady comes in smiling and hunches her shoulders at me and walks away. Finally, everyone is present. I'm formally introducing myself, "Hello, my name is Coach Archie." Before I can get into my introduction, a hand goes up. I said, "Yes Ma'am," and the young lady asked if she could go to the bathroom. I said sure, and the entire team escorted her to the restroom. Mrs. Anderson steps out of her office and asks, "Where are the girls?" I said, "Bathroom break," and she smiled and went back into her office. I realized that many of these girls had never played basketball before, and I've never coached girls in anything – OMG! Moving forward, after hard work and determination from the ladies, and myself learning twelve different personalities, the girls and I were ready. The season was going well until we met what turned out to be the school's rival. My team was Excellence Christian Eagles vs. Holy Trinity. Well, we lost that game by at least 20 points.

I wanted to do something real special for the girls because they had been working so hard during practice and all season. I decided to rent them a stretch limousine. I asked a good friend of mine who had a limo and service to transport my Lady Eagles to the Holy Trinity game, and his answer was yes. I was so excited that I was able to pull this off. The day of the game, I told the girls that we were riding a bus to the game, as this would have been a treat as well, due to the fact that we normally carpooled to and from games.

I asked the limo driver to stall while I pretended to be upset that the bus had not arrived and we would be late. Parents began making arrangements to carpool. While the parents were getting the transportation together, the limo driver pulled up. Prior to him pulling up, a couple of girls kept checking to see if the bus had arrived. I gathered the girls up so that we could pray before we departed for our game. What happened next was priceless. I had the Principal, Joe Crisp, announce that the bus was outside. When we opened the gym door to go outside, you should have seen the excitement in the girls' faces. They kept yelling, "Oh my gosh! Oh my gosh! Is this for us?" Mario had the red carpet out that stretched from the limo to the gym door. There were staff, parents and other coaches taking pictures of the girls as they all jumped up and down and ran around screaming.

Maybe that's where all their energy was left, back at the school. The limo driver advised the Lady Eagles that they could have whatever they wanted that was stocked in the beverage compartment. There were sodas, juices, chips and other snacks. My little cousin, who played on the team, said to me, "Coach Archie, did you say we could have whatever we want? And I said, "Yes you can." The cameras continued to flash. I told the girls to make sure they think about the game. That was probably the last thing on their mind.

How could anyone turn a positive experience for 4th, 5th and 6th graders into something negative? Some say the girls lost because of the limo ride; Coach Archie was showing off and trying to make the other coaches look bad. I bet he will never do that again. Well, I am a coach that promotes God first, academics second and then athletics. And bottom line is something nice was done for the Lady Eagles. They enjoyed it and that is what matters. After the lost, the only thing these young ladies thought about was the limo ride. So I made a promise to my girls that if we see them again, we would win.

Playoff time was upon us. We won the first game by 10 points. The next game we won by one point at the buzzer. Now, with a chance to make school history, we face our rival. The girl's games in the beginning of the season were normally the first game, but as the season went on the girls became pretty popular in the school so they would always get a crowd. On Championship day, they moved our game to the second game due to the buzz. On that day, I felt something and the girls were treated like queens. They had their own private room with sandwich platters, fruit bowls, water, and juices. They were treated like school celebrities. A lot of pictures were being taken and all this was two hours before the game. As game time approached, I saw the opposing team and coach and she gave me a look of confidence. I paused for a second and told her that the team she will see tonight is a different team. She smiled and said, "Sure coach."

My pep talk to my girls was one for the ages. I wish I had written it down. I lined the girls up to prepare them for their entry. When these girls entered the gym, you would have thought it was a high school or college championship game. The gym erupted with people stomping, cheering, clapping and yelling out the girls' names. It was unbelievable. As the girls began their pre-game drills, you could sense that they were nervous. I was nervous. I kept talking to my team, trying to take their focus off of the opponent. My girls kept looking at the other team. With about two minutes until game time, I removed the girls from the gym to have one more pep talk.

And my famous words to the girls were, "You're not little girls right now. You are basketball players." Then we came close together for prayer and we headed back to the gym. This time the Lady Eagles had a look of "we can do this." So I called out my starting line up and said let's do this right. Right before the tip-off, I pulled Kennedy aside for her separate pep talk. She was a special player. She never complained and always gave me 110%. I said, "Kennedy, we may never get this opportunity again for some of your teammates. This may be the last time for them to play for a championship." With a little smile on her face, she says to me "Coach, we're going to be okay."

The game started and the defense we've been working on all year has been working well. All I wanted was for the game to be close in the last period, and it was. I saw fatigue start to set in on several of my girls. The first one to falter was my little cousin. She was tired and crying and raising her hand to be taken out of the game. I told her in my stern coaching voice, "Suck it up. I can't take you out right now. Your team needs you." Somehow, miraculously, she pulled herself together and grabbed three crucial rebounds. Then Diamond and Mariah, my two little spark plugs had their best game of the season. They applied so much pressure to opposing team guards.

Both of them looked over to me, hoping that I would ask them if they needed a break. That's when my assistant coach Mike came to me and said, "If you are going to give them a break, now is the time." So I pulled the two little ones out, and as they were about to sit on the bench, I told them not to get too comfortable. I don't think 15 seconds had passed before I kneeled down in front of them and in my coaches voice I said, "Now is not time to be sitting down." With a fatigued look, they both nodded their heads in agreement. I said, Get back in the game."

As soon as they got back in the game, Mariah took the ball from the opposing team and passed to Diamond for a score. With the clock running down and up by one point, I think the most crucial rebound came when Wesley boxed out and grabbed the rebound like Charles Barkley. She took the ball and fell to the floor. While she was falling to the floor, I called a timeout. With about 30 seconds left in the game, I told the girls to protect the ball and to keep it in the guards' hands. The gymnasium was going crazy with the home crowd sensing a victory. The next chain of events had the entire gym on the edge of their seats.

When we passed the ball in, Mariah got it with the clock winding down. The next pass was taken by the other team and my heart dropped to my feet. With ten seconds left, the other team called a timeout. We only led by one point with ten seconds left in the game. So I had twelve little girls looking at me for guidance. With numerous expressions on their faces, I said, "Ladies, no matter what happens in the next 10 seconds, I want you to know that I love each and every one of you. So let's go back out there and win the game." The other team passed the ball in and they have a set play. All I could remember after that was the best shooter being left all alone in the corner.

The clock had five seconds, four seconds. Someone get on her. The clock had three seconds, two seconds and a shot went up. One second and the ball hit the rim. Game over. When the clock hit 0 seconds, everyone ran out of the bleachers and stormed the floor. We're talking about an elementary school basketball game. I've never seen anything like that, other than when an unranked team beats a ranked team in college basketball. My assistant coach hugged me so hard, and he had tears of joy. I must admit I was crying, too.

Our team made God, me and the school extremely proud. I want to take time out to give thanks to Principal Joe Crisp, Athletic Director, Mrs. Shemia Anderson, Rev. Daniel T. Mangrum and Rev. Sabrina A. Mangrum for all the prayers, love and support given to me from Excellence Christian School. It was an honor to represent your school. Thanks to my Assistant Coach, Mike Arnett. Congrats Ladies. (Alicia Arnett, Kendall Ballentine, Moriah Crisp, Kennedi Harris, Evan Jackson, Faith Johnson, Diamond Mangrum, Natalie Richardson, Phebe Simpson, Zana Stewart, Justice Westmoreland, Leah White, Wesley Young.)

A MEMORY THAT WILL LAST A LIFETIME.

Chapter 5
TAMIKA STORY

I remember coaching one year when my team mom was running late. Luckily the games were also running behind schedule, so I wasn't worrying about it at the time. The issue was the team mom usually has the player identification cards, birth certificates and game check-in verifications. You are supposed to have these items in our league by halftime of the preceding game. This process is done just to ensure fair play amongst the teams and to make sure children are who they say they are.

On this particular day, my team mom was seriously late, so I tried reaching out to her by phone and did not get an answer. I tried to text her, but still no response. Now, I started to worry because it was uncharacteristic of her to not respond and the items she had were very important. By league rules, without the team's identification items, the team will forfeit the game. Now, its twenty minutes before game time and the parents and coaches that know how the process works are starting to get a little frustrated, some more than others.

So I reached out to her once again, and she answered this time. It was obvious that there was something wrong or something had happened. My first words to my team mom were "Are you okay?" She started talking and I could hear her voice start to crack. She started apologizing over and over again because she also knew the importance of the book that contained the player's identification cards. So I asked her if she was close, and she started crying, saying sorry coach, I made a wrong turn and I'm not sure where I am. I could tell as each minute passed she started getting even more upset. At this time to me, the game was secondary. I didn't want to put any more pressure on her.

By now the game before our game had ended and all of the parents and coaches were questioning me about the player's identification cards. Now, I'm trying to calm my team mom down and respond to my angry parents. What bothered me the most about the situation was the fact that everyone's only focus was about the IDs and not the welfare of the team mom who was clearly upset. I heard things like "well if she can't be responsible, I can do it," and "this doesn't make any sense," and "she should have never had the IDs in the first place."

With all of this going on, I pulled the opposing team coach to the side and asked if he could please bear with us since we were the last game of the day. I advised him that my team mom was about 15 minutes away and he simply said, "No problem." So with that settled with the opposing coach, I began to get my team together again to stay loose and get warmed up. Once I thought everything was straightened out, the team mom arrived and before she got out of the car I told her to get herself together before she exited her vehicle. She continued to apologize and I said, "No need to apologize."

Now, the IDs had arrived. Of course there is always one parent that just won't let things go. I had reached my breaking point and I simply said to this parent, "You do realize that at the end of the day, it's really not that serious." The sole purpose should be for the children to have fun.

Chapter 6

THE DEQUAN STORY

It was a beautiful Saturday morning, and it was game day. While I was preparing my football team to get ready for our opponent, I do my usual pre-game warm-up with my team. Prior to each game, both teams have to check their players in to make sure all the players had their ID's. As I give my team their instructions for preparation for the game, I realized we hadn't checked in, and the reason was that the opposing team didn't seem to have enough players to start with a legal line-up. So, doing what Coach Archie does, even though I had folks in my ear telling me that the other team is not ready and if they don't get a couple more players, then we should take a forfeit, meaning since the other doesn't have a legal line-up to start with, my team would get the win.

For those that know me, I'm not an advocate for punishing or penalizing players; or should I say, not awarding them the opportunity to compete. So I would usually stall for the other team, against some people's wishes, then I would have to reiterate that this day and football activity is for the student athletes. I noticed that the other team had at least enough players to compete with. I went over to the opposing coach and asked if they were ready. Now mind you, I gave them an additional 30 minutes to get players. This coach had the audacity to say with malice and anger in his voice, along with an evil look, ARE YOU READY! I said "wow" to myself and turned around and walked away to get back to my team, with different things running through my head. I had to pause for a second to reiterate to myself my purpose and vision for what I do with our youth isn't the same consistent vision and purpose that the vast majority of coaches have.

So now I'm back with my team. I gather my players, and at this time, I could have used that situation to fire me up and motivate my team. I will never allow negative anger or non-competitive anger take over me while I'm dealing with our youth. While I have all my players together, it's time to pray. I would always start the prayer by saying WHO'S FATHER, and then the team would proceed with the Lord's Prayer by saying Our Father and together we all say the Lord's Prayer. After the prayer, my team administrator Mrs. Tonya Bridgeman approached me stating that the Head coach of the opposing team had a special needs child, and they wanted to do a ceremonial play for the young man. So the coach asked if we could line up our defense on the field along with his offense so that he could have the young man run the football, and I agreed to do this.

I advised my players and coaches on what was about to happen, and I advised my players, by no means make an attempt to tackle the young man. So both teams line up on the field. My team was on defense, and the young man was at the running back position for his team. Now everyone is set, and the quarterback begins his cadence and the running back is ready and waiting. While his helmet was as big as his body this real small child with the heart of a lion was ready to go. The quarterback hands the child the ball, and there he goes running like the only thing that matters right now is that he has been given the opportunity to be like everyone else. Some folks had tears of joy on their faces and other people were cheering, jumping up and down and screaming his name. The energy and love this child received was awesome.

After he ran the ball in the end zone about 40 yards, all the players met him in the end zone. They were patting him on his helmet and his back and shaking his hand. And I'm talking about both teams were in the end zone with him. I forgot to state that the coach told me that he had asked other teams to do this, and in most cases he got resistance. I just shook my head. I told the coach I was honored to do it, and it gave me more life lessons to share with my student athletes. The parents of the young man for that one moment in time were able to celebrate their child as a football player.

So the following season, my team Mom/administrator and Coach Rick Taylor, who is a dynamite gentleman and also the founder and President of the Patuxent Rhino's youth organization that offers football, both flag and tackle, along with cheerleading, basketball and mentoring. Coach Rick Taylor is a man of God and is doing great things for our student athletes. On a hot evening in July they both were approached by a woman asking them to introduce her to Coach Moshe. Coach Moshe is another dynamic coach in our organization that just gets it.

And the "it" is, he puts God first and he knows everything else will fall in its proper place. Now the woman stated that she spoke with Coach Moshe via email concerning her twelve-year-old son. They told her that he was conducting practice and if she wanted to register her son that I could help her. She proceeded to state that she needed to talk to the head of the organization concerning her son and that he had special circumstances that she did not discuss with Coach Moshe in the email because she wanted to plead her son's case in person to give him a fair chance. The conversation was enlightening. It was pleaded that her son has a disability, but he was much more than that, and if given the chance he just wanted to be with children his age and to put on a Rhino uniform.

Being moved by such a story, Mrs. Bridgeman decided that he should be with our team so that he could get the experience and never forget it. Coach Rick Taylor started to inform her that he was sorry, but could not guarantee that he would get the experience he was looking for. So Mrs. Bridgeman pulled Rick aside and asked him if we could do this because her heart would not let her live with him not getting that one wish of being with his peers in the sport that he loved. Rick gave Mrs. Bridgeman the go ahead and told her that he had to have the credentials and we must let the teams that we play be aware of his disability. Mrs. Bridgeman then ensured the man that he would be okay, and she introduced the young man. He and Mrs. Bridgeman hugged and smiled and told him let's go and meet my brother, the best coach in the world, and he laughed and hugged Mrs. Bridgeman real tight.

That was the start of our beautiful friendship with the Connelly family. I remember telling Tonya that I can't accept any more children or add any more children to my roster. I also explained to her that I don't care how good they appeared to be or even if he was stamped as a must-have child. So with this understanding already in place, I can recall Tonya walking towards me with a child by her side. I know that this wasn't someone that was interested in football. I figured it was someone Tonya knew or the child was just hanging out until one of his siblings or friends finished practice. As she got closer to me, she had this look on her face, and I immediately started shaking my head no, I can't do it.

Tonya said, "Just hear me out," and started explaining the situation. Once she said that this young man was a special needs child, I told her, "Enough said, I will make a spot for him." When she introduced the young man to me, he was very shy and distant. I advised him man that if he wants to play football, I would do everything in my power to make sure his experience on my team will be fun and productive. At the time, he didn't have much to say. He just kind of looked at me and smiled. I also met his parents. They were very thankful and they appreciated the fact that I was giving their son the opportunity to be one of the guys. So I told my team, from this day forward, they were to treat Dequan extra special, and that they did.

Dequan became the team's favorite player. I assured Mom and Dad that I would treat him like the rest of my players. Before practice and at the end of practice, my team would say a prayer. I would select an individual to say the end of practice prayer, but at the start of practice we say the Lord's Prayer. So, one practice I chose Dequan to lead us in prayer. Mind you, the young man never opens his mouth to speak. One of my players said, "Come on, Coach Archie, you know Dequan doesn't like to talk." I called Dequan again to come to the front of the team to lead us in prayer, and even Dequan had a look on his face like he was surprised that I had called his name. Once his teammates realized I was serious, they all started to encourage Dequan to speak, "Come on Dequan. You can do it." Dequan slowly made his way to the front of the team. I said, "Go ahead, son. You can do this. Just speak from your heart."

Needless to say, a few seconds went by, maybe even several minutes went by, and Dequan still hadn't uttered a word. This is a child who, to my knowledge, hasn't said a word all season. What stood out to me is how his teammates all kept their heads down waiting patiently for Dequan to say something--anything would have been timely. So, I whispered in Dequan's ear, "Allow the Lord to come into your heart." Amazingly, at that time, Dequan began to mumble several things. I once again whispered in his ear and told him to say, "In Jesus Name we pray, Amen." Out of nowhere, those words came out of Dequan's mouth loud and clear; not mumbles, and his teammates were in shock and disbelief.

So as the season progressed, I wanted to stay on track with his mom's wishes, I had to figure out a way to incorporate him into the system so he can be a part of this football experience. I decided to put him in one game for the kickoff team. I figured that would be safe and fun. To see him on the kick off team and see him run down the field with a smile on his face was priceless. After one of my practices, his dad advised me that he had been working with Dequan on his kicking, and that I should give him a shot at trying to kick off. His dad did say it was a work in progress, and that even though he wasn't kicking it far; he was consistently kicking it straight without any hesitation. I told his dad I would use him as kicker. I figured his dad didn't believe I would, so at the next practice when I called for the kick-off team, Daniel who was my all-purpose student-athlete ran on the field to kick. I called on Dequan to replace him, and once again my team, along with my coaching staff, thought I was playing. When I made that switch, you would think that they should know me and my decision making by now. The way this would work was Daniel would place the ball on the kick tee for Dequan and Dequan's first kick went 30 yards, which may not seem impressive, but in my scheme of special teams, it was perfect. You see my philosophy in youth's sports during kick-offs is to kick the ball short, not deep, and to the other team's weakness. Let me tell you that every one of his kicks was perfect in practice. So the day came when Dequan got the opportunity to kick the ball in a real game. No one took me serious, not even my coaching staff.

So now it's game day, and what made this extra special was that this particular game was against one of our top opponents in the league. The referees asked for the captains, and on this day I sent Malik, Daniel and my secret weapon Dequan out for the coin toss. Usually the coin toss is a formality and no one really pays attention to who goes out; they only pay attention to the results. So you can hear some chatter in reference to Dequan going out for the toss, and the look on his Mom's face was priceless. The following sequence of events is why I thought it was important to tell this young man's story. You see, the magnitude of something like this changes lives and people's mind-sets. So I bring my team in for the pre-game prayer, and by the way we won the toss, so I elected to kick. As we finish the prayer, Lil Martin shouted, "Rhinos on 3 … 1, 2, 3 Rhinos."

I told the kicking team to go out, and at the time I held Dequan beside me until the last possible moment, and of course my very attentive parents start yelling, "Coach, you only have 10 people out there." So I leaned over to Dequan and I asked him, "Son, are you ready?" He gave me the smile of a lifetime. I told him go out there and give me a good kick, just like in practice. As he trotted on the field, you could hear the Rhino's parents and fans saying, "It's Dequan," while others were saying, "What is Coach Archie doing? This game is important." The only thing that was important to me was giving that young man an opportunity to contribute and be normal like his other teammates. As he's trotting on the field, all his teammates started encouraging him and giving him love. Daniel was the director of my kick-off operations. Daniel placed the ball on the kicking tee for Dequan and told him where to kick, too, and the rest of the story was one out of a Hollywood script. Dequan kicked the ball to the opposing team player. The ball took a favorable bounce and hit the opposing player in the chest, and our team recovered the ball to start the game off and Dequan's kicking debut.

Needless to say his Mom, alongside several other parents, began to cry real tears of joy. All you could hear was Dequan's Mom saying, "Oh my goodness. My baby, my baby." The remainder of our season was successful, which landed us in Orlando, FL with the opportunity to compete for the AAU National Football Championship. Dequan proved to be a special football player that continued to do his part to help our team. I will never forget that season or my secret weapon, Dequan.

Chapter 7
MESSAGE TO THE YOUTH

If you're reading this portion of the book for the first time, I hope that you pass this on or encourage someone else to read this as well. If for some reason you haven't read the book at all and someone asked you to read this section, you need to thank him or her when you're done because that person cares about you.

I want you to take time out to think of all the things you've done wrong, and then ask yourself if you were aware that they were wrong when you did these things. Then ask yourself, did you do these things even when someone told you not to or did you do these things because you saw someone else do it.

While you're thinking and reading, I'm going to make an attempt to help you with this and you can thank Coach Archie later. You see, without your parents there would be no you, meaning you wouldn't exist. Without your grandparents, your mom and dad wouldn't exist. You should find time to give your family members a hug and tell them you love them, even apologize for the things you've done wrong. This should be extended to sisters, brothers, aunts, uncles, cousins and your guardian.

How many times has someone used these words: academics, respect for others, watch your image, be a leader not a follower, always stay focused, what are your plans for the future, do you have any goals, be responsible, you should always have good manners, say your prayers before you go to bed, do your homework, complete all assignments, are you saving money? Just imagine if you were to do all of these, where you would be as a person, but I challenge you to do all these. You see this represents the blueprint or road map for your life. Going to school shouldn't be something you look at as being boring; too long, or something you take for granted. You're not going to school for anyone but yourself. You see school and learning are life. While in school, you should work on being the best you can be and not playing around or talking to kids that you know don't care about learning.

Be a leader for yourself so you can follow yourself. You should never use profanity, and you should always make sure you're properly dressed. Stop doing what you see everyone else doing, and just do the opposite when you know what he or she is doing is wrong. Set goals to find out what you want to be, or what you want to do after high school. When you're talking to your friends, start having conversations about what you're going to do today, tomorrow, this month, this year that is going to help you get prepared for life. Let me leave you with this: The same respect you give your coaches, I want you to give your parents, teachers, and everyone else that cares about you and that are trying to make you the best young lady or young man that you can possibly be.

Coach Archie will continue to pray, mentor, and support every young lady or young man that is in need of an extra push.

Chapter 8
OTHER VOICES

I hope that my experiences have helped to further your understanding of my methods and ways in which you can help a child gain self-confidence in all aspects of his or her life. The following dialogue that I had with many through the years may also shed some light on strengthening our bonds and support with our youth. Why do we praise our youth athletes more for athletics and less for academics?

"It's all about access. Sports have long been seen by our community as a way to "make it." It's changing now, but we are still programmed with that mentality." – Parent

"We want to see our children excel at the things that we see them perform well in. Something as commonly emphasized as sports gets more attention than academics. Academic talents go unnoticed because they are never exposed and thus properly nurtured. More emphasis should be placed on academics, but parents have to step up." – Parent

"Most humans have a need for instant gratification. Scores on the court/field are more tangible, more frequent and more widely communicated than scores in the classroom. I believe this is the basis for the 'meal ticket' mentality." – Parent

"You have to get the scores in the classroom before you can do any scoring on the court/field. That's why they are student athletes. I know in the NCAA there are academic all-American teams for the student-athletes who maintain a high GPA during their season, which is very hard to do. I don't think it is anything wrong with a child aspiring to be a professional athlete. As long as they know in order to play or do any extracurricular activity, you have to get the grade." - Parent

"Little Johnny will get pulled off of the team if his grades are not where they should be and I don't mean the C average that the school requires to stay one. It's important that we allow our children to express their physical talents but not lose sight – the goal is college and the talent may just be ONE of the spring boards to get the child there...becoming a Pro should only be considered the bonus." – Parent

"As a coach, I see that we have a lot of adults who enable and promote this attitude and behavior in our youth. They are given a pass from the classroom as well as on the playing fields. Academics are never pressed on these children unless they run into an educator who doesn't care what the coach says. I have seen this time and time again when a child has been afforded a so-called chance for extra credit not to improve in the classroom but to stay eligible to play sports. Until parents, educators and coaches start taking the academic part of a child's development more seriously, we will continue to produce children who can catch and dunk a ball but cannot count their money." - Coach

WHAT DO YOU SAY TO A YOUTH PARTICIPATING IN SPORTS, WHEN HE OR SHE HAS GIVEN THEIR BEST AND THEIR PARENTS STILL GIVE THEM A HARD TIME ON THEIR EFFORTS?

"I think you should allow your youth player to be disappointed before trying to cheer them up. I also think a player also needs to know that they can fail and still be supported. Parents should be the ones

giving their child that support and encouragement, telling them that with good, hard work they can be successful. This encourages them to think that they can do anything in their life – particularly when it comes from their own parents! Give only constructive, positive compliments. Strive for excellence and perfection!" – Coach

"You tell them to continue playing the game at the best of their ability. I would also address the parent(s) and simply let them know that what they may see as the child not putting forth his/her best effort may be the kid's best attempt at that time. You want to encourage children not discourage them. Some children are simply just late bloomers, so every child will not play at the same level. Some will stand out and maybe even go on to the next level and some will go on to do other things in life. That's just the way it is, that's just the way it goes. I think parents that push their children to the extreme are trying to live out their own past through their child. Essentially, let them know you are proud of their best effort, but most importantly just go out there and have fun!" – Coach

"You tell them the truth! You've done a great job, and I feel like you gave it your best and that's all I can ask for! You tell the child to keep his head up and don't allow anyone to discourage them and keep trying as hard as they can. If you feel like you did the best you can do, then you achieved your goal and be confident in what you've done." Coach

"Tell them to continue to give their best and it will pay off in the end. Tell the youth that your parents are hard on you because they don't want you to suffer from the consequences that they went through." – Parent

"In their lives, they will hear many voices in their head – role models, parents, coaches, etc. Our job as adults is to be that positive and encouraging voice that they hear." – Parent

Do you prefer that youth coaches be nice, tough, or mean while coaching your children?

Decisive, firm, fair and reasonable. A coach, like any other teacher, should be in charge but strong enough to know that they do not know everything. They should be able to accept suggestions that differ from their thoughts if the suggestion is supported with the facts and delivered with respect." - Parent

"There is a time and place for each. The trick is finding the proper balance." - Parent

"I prefer nice and tough. There is no reason for the meanness. Some coaches believe they are trying to live their childhood dreams through these children." – Parent

"Ain't nothing wrong with teaching a lil discipline." – Parent

"Can I choose none of the above? A coach is supposed to be an instructor, and an effective coach will be a motivator thus kind of eliminating the need to be any of those characteristics… (Whispering) but I really want a nice coach for my babies." – Parent

"While attempting to achieve the goals of the team, each player has to be treated as an individual. Direction can be given in multiple ways, but it is the coaches' responsibility to nurture each player with a different style. Remember they are still children and should be praised for each accomplishment." - Parent

"I think you should be all of the above. Each emotion has a time or place on the court. The feelings associated with the emotion are defined by the player. The child feels that you as a parent are mean at different times – my mean coach taught me the most and looking back he wasn't mean – I was stubborn." – Parent

"I believe the coaches need to be all of the above! You as a coach have to know your children and be able to evaluate the appropriate measures to go through or what to do better. Know when to hold them and when to fold them. You just have to be able to relate what you're doing to their parents. All children are different!" – Coach

"I think they need to be understanding of a child's ability and help the child meet his or her full ability by providing coaching of the sport and not take what they can or cannot do as personal failure." – Parent

"Firm and rational with their expectations." – Parent

"I say tough because they world is tough. You have to prepare the children to leave the nest. That is what you are supposed to be doing from the time they are born. Our children are molded by the kinds of things and people in their life. Being nice makes them soft and not prepared for the harshness of the world. Being mean just makes them mean and cold to everything. We have to always remember children are our future and to think about what kind of child we are releasing into our society." – Parent

"Tough love is best." – Parent

"All three. If your child plays sports you want them to be tough. It gets even tougher in high school and college." – Parent

"Depends on the age. My five year old's coach gives positive reinforcement while other team's coaches were yelling at them... My son's team only lost one game in the entire season. It's discouraging if they are too young. If coaching a child older than 9 they should be firm." – Parent

"Firm, but fair. A coach has to be able to evaluate a kid's skill set as it pertains to the activities they are involved in. That's where the fair comes in. Also understanding that will assist with being firm.

Parents have to be able to evaluate a coach's ability to communicate with their child, to make sure the child understands the information being conveyed to them. A confused young mind can be dangerous."
– Parent

"Depending on the ages of the children. You don't want to hurt their spirits. Tough is always good. Mean is unacceptable. Fair is what is acceptable and expected." – Parent

What do you think about a head coach that plays his or her child often no matter what the child's skill level is?

"There needs to be some level of objectivity about skill level. If the child is good, which is more likely the case, it is fine. If the child isn't good, then I resort to blaming the parent/coach who spent so much time with other children that they couldn't get their own child up to speed with whatever sport it is…" – Parent

"You know that's one of the major problems with the youth athletics now. Nepotism. Some coaches make the mistake of crowding the line between parent and coach and forget about the objectives of coaching youth athletics. Teaching competitive spirits though fair play and executive of acquired skills. You lose all of that when the coach's child gets the bulk of the time and the bulk of the coaching. It has been my experience that other children lose their desire to compete when they know the deck is stacked against them. Coming from a sports background, it was never a practice to showcase a certain child, especially the coach's child. Coaches used to allow the children on each team to compete and fight for the opportunity to play and that they weren't going to put anything less than the best team possible on the field." – Parent

"Personally I think a lot of parent/coaches play their own children because they believe their children have grasped the desired play/skill more than the other children because they practice with their child

outside of normal practices. In their mind they think that their child can show their teammates how to get it done." – Parent

"Playing time should be earned, not a given because of who you are related to. Favoritism should not play a part." – Parent

"I have mixed emotions about this topic. If a coach's child has skills (i.e. the best player on the team) I'm sure most would not have a problem with the kid's playing time. However, if the child's skill level is poor, then we scream "bloody murder" when the child makes a mistake. Honestly, I think people only have a real problem with the coach's child playing if the team is losing." – Parent

Chapter 9
My Final Thoughts

Being a parent, coach and mentor has opened up many doors for me, exposing me to a wide variety of households--some good, some bad, single parents and some with both parents, but only one parent are active. I often hear people say that fathers should play a more active role in their children's lives. When in fact, there are a lot of fathers involved, but their involvement is what one needs to question. There are many fathers that are doing more damage to our student athletes by being involved than those fathers that are not involved. But I will talk about this more in detail in my next book.

So in closing, parents let's show our student athletes love and support all of the time, win or lose. Let's start respecting the people that coach our youth, and if you don't like something, talk directly to the coach and the parents in reference to your complaints. Find out what organization or coach has a place for academic growth and spiritual growth. Coaches give your vision to your athletes and parents, and stick to it. Provide an atmosphere where all of our student athletes can get something out of the season. Most importantly, we as coaches are put on pedestals in the eyes of our student athletes, so let's be mindful of the influence we have. Our image stays in a student athlete's mind. My motto is: *"The Mentor with patience out of this world, and a drive to make a difference in every young man and young woman life."* We keep fighting, even when the parent or parents have run out of fight. I personally want to thank God for making this my purpose in life--serving our youth. I hope that something in this book inspired you and motivated change in you and gave you a different perspective on youth sports. And at the end of the day, let's keep it structured, let's keep it fair, and most importantly, let's keep it FUN!!!

Random Thoughts and Stuff

- A referee said to me once, "I've been doing your games for the past couple of years. Man, you're unique in the way you handle your teams, and if I had a son, I would want you to be his coach." It's comments like that that lets me know I'm not just reaching the children, but the adults as well.

- One of my past football players called me and simply said "thanks." I hadn't talked to this young man in two years. He told me that one of my messages stuck in his head, and he thinks it may have saved his life.

- Rode past a popular shoe store after work at 1AM and people were in line. Rode past the store heading back to work at 7AM and the line had tripled in numbers of young people waiting for the store to open to purchase a pair of new sneakers – "new old shoes" that were just released. Teenagers and adults were in line. Why? We should be encouraging our youth and parents to line up for church, voting, SATs and school events.

- Dads stop focusing on making your sons football tough when you know your son is not. Spend more time on giving him wisdom to prepare him for life.

- Let's not forget that the devil is always busy, especially these days. He's working on our youth. So when your child goes left instead of right with his or her education or life choices, let's not get angry. Instead, get on your knees with them that night and pray together. Parent and child praying together is priceless.

Chapter 10
Testimonials

The title "Coach" is an understatement when it comes to Archie Beslow. In the short time that we have been a part of the Patuxent Rhino family, he has proven to be an inspirational speaker, teacher, motivator, life coach and even a comedian. His practices, such as group prayer before and after each gathering and reading before contact, convey a strong message that spirituality and education are priorities. In addition, he emphasizes the importance of responsibility, values and character. He drives home the fact that these are all essential elements in becoming productive men.

We adore the fact that the Coach uses football, a language that many boys understand and enjoy as a metaphoric vehicle, to teach our children life-long lessons. He shows them that their experiences on the field are very similar to life's experiences and challenges. In football, as in life, you'll face knockdowns, tackles and sometimes get benched. He stresses that it's your response to those setbacks that brings out the best in each of them. I am confident that the seeds he is currently planting in our boys will surely blossom as they develop into young men. He lets them know that they must work hard but that it's ok to have fun.

Coach Archie's genuine love for the children far exceeds his love for the sport, which I believe contributes greatly to his teams' success. He leads by example and his smiling face and encouraging attitude are truly contagious. He has surrounded himself with a support team of coaches and team moms with similar demeanors and beliefs, creating an atmosphere of sheer positivity. Coach Archie is the epitome of a great coach, and we are proud to be members of the Patuxent Rhino Family. -- Denise Briscoe-Lee, mother of 12U team member Jalen Lee

"When a parent gets their children involved in sports, Coach Archie is the type of coach you dream of your child having. As a coach, he teaches his players the skills necessary to improve their competitiveness on the field or the court. He sees every child as a diamond in the rough with the potential to be a Hope diamond. Not only does he prepare your child to compete, he reinforces life skills like hard work, being a team player and resiliency which helps them mature into young adults while also having fun. He is a mentor who continually affirms the motto of "Do The Right Thing" to his players, coaching staff and parents by emphasizing the importance of getting an education and being a responsible individual. In his spare time, he visits his players' teachers to ensure getting good grades is the primary goal of his athletes. He also spends his time giving back to the community by public speaking to youth groups and aspiring coaches. Coach Archie sincerely cares for the children he coaches as if they were his own children. It is refreshing to see a coach that cares about the development of their players athletically and as an individual first and not about their win-loss record or accolades from their successful teams. I have had the pleasure of being an assistant coach to Coach Archie. I cannot think of another coach or a better person I would follow on a field or court to teach children the skills to win a game but also the skills to win in life." -- Cheryl

I'm pleased to be a part of this team, our coach is so amazing. He has managed to take our children to a whole new level outside of football. The boys were so excited to share their readings with their teammates after the mandatory ReadB4Contact time. Coach Archie extends his mentoring to our children by going to their schools, receiving their phone calls any time of the day, and providing encouragement on the field. He has dedicated his time to our children and we appreciate it. -- Tonya Bridgman (Team Mom)

Many words and phrases can be used to describe Coach Archie, but there are none to truly explain his character. Humble, loving, caring, trustworthy, gentle … the list goes on infinitely. God sent each and every one of us to fulfill a purpose in life, and I can say with no doubt in my mind that Coach Archie was sent with a particularly special one. He inspires me to do my best not only academically and athletically, but also in life period. Because at the end of the day, if you haven't given it everything you've got, then it was a waste of time. Every night I say my prayers and ask God to protect my friends and family. Coach Archie taught me that my enemies should be on the list too. When you look at him, you may see him with a t-shirt, jeans, tennis shoes and maybe even a hat. You think to yourself, "he's just a regular guy," but for me I see him with angel wings and a halo. -- Braedon Domino

Raising children is a difficult job; they say it takes a village. I used to think I could do it all on my own and then came those teenage years. When I brought my son Jacoby out to James Madison middle school, I just wanted him to have a chance to show off his skills and win. Now that we are with the Rhinos and Coach Archie, things are different. He has been a positive influence on Jacoby, both on and off the field. He puts God and family first, and no game is more important that school. I feel like he is there whenever we need him and he is never too busy. I am proud to call Coach Archie my friend and one day I hope I can help him like he has helped my family and me. -- Wren Lewis

Coach Archie, you've been like a second parent to me. Best football coach I've ever had. I'm happy that you have taken the time to check on me in school and one on one outside of regular practices. I know I can always call you if I need help or just to say what's up. You will always be a part of my life and I just want to say thanks. -- E.J.

Our initial meeting wasn't idealistic! I didn't know what to expect from the "Coach." After a while that changed. Talking and seeing how you interacted with the children gave me insight on you as a person. I could see that you were not just there for the sport but that you genuinely cared about the children. You were concerned with how they did in school, you were teaching them life lessons through sports. Having experienced your persona in football and basketball, it was evident that you were a different type of coach. I'm thankful for the time you've taken with my son. You came into his life when he needed something to get him turned around and focused in the right direction. You are indeed a special individual and I hope you will always use your God-given talent to affect the lives of young people! -- Cheryl Joppy

Coach Archie, I wanted to extend my appreciation to you for your time, energy, loyalty, commitment, dedication, support, obligation, and love you show to you Student-Athletes. Over the years you have coached and mentored hundreds of boys and girls. I think you've played an extremely positive role in many. Coach that actually makes school visits shadows the Student-Athletes to their classes, sit in their classes, take notes and report your findings to the parents. Who does that? Well, Coach Archie does that! My prayer is that other Coaches will follow your lead and help make our children successful in life, not just sports. You are greatly appreciated! -- Blessing, From a Parent

Archie is that rare mentor/coach who uses life skills and lessons to teach and motivate our youth. I can honestly say that my son that is now 17 still refers to the core principles and values learned from his Coach Archie. Everything Archie gives to our youth comes from the right place … He's passionate and generally cares, not to mention the sacrifices made just to see young people excel. I'm looking forward to purchasing this book for my son. God Bless You, Brother! -- Derick Boyd

You never coached my son and you probably don't remember this. During the time we worked together as my daughter fought for her little life (RIP Tiffany); you taught me how to laugh in spite of my situation. Your kind of spirit and your laughter many times was how I made it through the day. You never know whose life your positive spirit has touched. Thanks for all the encouragement you have through laughter. -- Sincerely, Creela

Coach Archie is one of the most talented coaches I have ever observed. He knows how to motivate his players to play their best while keeping them loose so that they are having fun. His exceptional people skills allow him to relate to all the players and get them to work together as a team under his direction. Coach Archie uses sports to build character and instill life skills. -- Daniel Mangrum

Coach Archie has been a big role model for me. He always motivates me to do my best in everything I do. I can always count on him when I am feeling down, angry or discouraged. No matter what it is, I can count on Coach Archie. Thanks to him, I was motivated to play football and thanks to his support, I'm now working towards a full athletic scholarship to go to college. Coach Archie is like family. He will always support and care and most importantly love when you need it. He always compliments and motivates you to do your best and makes you feel great about yourself. To me Dr. Phil ain't got nothing on Coach Archie. Thank you for your positive support. -- Andre Parker

Coach Archie shows an innovative approach to mentoring and coaching together with careful communication with aggressive tone. Great leadership by explanation and example instead of anger. It's a rare quality in this day and time when parents try to live through their children. He's way more like a teacher than a coach. That's my main man making a difference. Way to go Cuzzo! -- David Pope

Coach Archie was the best coach I ever had while playing youth football. Not only did he care about how I performed on the field but mostly in the classroom. He would always check up on my grades and visit the school. -- Stephen Israel

In the 8th grade, my son played football and then basketball the same year with Coach Archie. In football, Coach led us to go undefeated, win the MD State Championship, and play in the National Championships. In basketball, we lost way more games than we won. But for both seasons, my son was the true winner because he was able to work with a coach that actually motivates without degrading, actually cares about the players, and has a true calling for mentoring. Coach Archie's main focus is not the scoreboard but in seeing that his players give their best on and off the field/court and assisting in whatever way to help them develop into respectful and productive people. Coach even sits in on his player's classes on his days off. He is an excellent role model that shows children how they too can use what they learn by participating in sports, apply it in the classroom, get an education, and make a good life for themselves. -- Sonday Kelly

"Shoot!!!" Coach Archie would tell us or me, in particular. I've known Coach Archie for four years and two of those years he was my basketball coach at Excellence Christian School. The first year he led us to a great championship game. Our team was made up of a group of girls who knew little about basketball or never played the game at all. I was one of those girls who never played. Coach Archie didn't give up on me; he saw my potential and kept working with me until I had the confidence to play. That championship game was so exciting. Our school gym was crowded and my whole team was nervous. After all, we were playing the championship game against a team that beat us good during the season. Now we had to face them again.

But Coach Archie was cool, calm and smiling as usual. I think we all were probably thinking why he is so calm, like it's an ordinary day or something. But he knew he had to make us comfortable. No matter how nervous we were, he kept encouraging us, never fussed at us to make us feel incapable but only raised his voice to ensure that we used the skills that he had taught us during every practice. He always made sure we understood how to do certain skills. He had so much patience with us because we were a group of prissy girls with a bunch of attitudes. He overlooked that and kept working with us because he wanted to make sure that we not only learned the game but enjoyed it as well. I think this is what makes him not just a good coach but also a great one. That championship game was the longest game of my life, but because of Coach Archie, we came out on top with a 13-12 win. I will never forget it. Ever since that season, Coach Archie has been like another dad. He has taken time to take me out to work on different sports training although he's no longer my coach. Soccer has always been my first sport so that's all I play now. When I get discouraged in soccer, I think back to Coach Archie telling me that I can do it and I push forward. He is one of the best coaches I have ever had because of his encouragement, trust, faith and devotion to helping the children he coaches. I know he will continue to do great things. Any parent will feel comfortable about him coaching their child. "Two thumbs up and a wink for Coach Archie." -- Kennedi Harris

Coach Archie-My Testimony is founded on the quote listed below. My son had been part of the Patuxent Rhinos organization for about three years before I met Coach Archie. What caused my motivation to meet him was I watched my son attempt to lose weight just so he could play for Coach, as I affectionately call him now. When I tell you my then 11 year old was so focused and disciplined about making the weight level so he could play for coach, and I had never seen my child that committed, or dedicated to a goal he had set for himself that I had to meet this Coach. Since meeting him, we have become brothers from other Mothers.

"When people believe in you, when they give you their time, their resources, their faith, and their trust, honor them by working your hardest. You should believe in yourself as much as they believe in you. If you are going to achieve excellence in big things, you develop the habit in little matters. Excellence is not an exception, it is a prevailing attitude. -- Preston Gerard Boyd

RECOGNIZED IN
WHO'S WHO IN PRINCE GEORGE'S COUNTY
TOP 125 INFLUENTIAL PEOPLE IN THE COUNTY
SEPTEMBER 2013

Author, Mentor, Youth Sports Coach, Motivational Speaker and decorated Police Officer, Archie R. Beslow has served on the Washington D.C. Metropolitan Police Department (MPD) since 1990, and has served on MPD's Executive Protection Unit since 1995, protecting DC Mayor Muriel Bowser and former D.C. Mayor's Marion Barry, Anthony Williams, Adrian Fenty and Vincent C. Gray.

A member of the Fraternal Order of Police, this decorated officer includes among his awards, an Achievement Medal and a Unit Citation. With a belief in discipline, Beslow, a.k.a Coach Archie, has a strong passion for preparing young athletes for sports and life through coaching and mentoring.

CEO of Coach 2 Mentor, Coach Archie mentors youth across the Metropolitan area by helping them develop, build confidence, and challenge their talents and abilities; encouraging them to thrive in sports and education; supporting parents in helping their children achieve success on and off the field of play (which includes home and school visits in the program); Read B4 Contact; and using a positive formula, P.A.S.S. (Prayer, Academics and Structure = Success).

Coach 2 Mentor Program

At Coach 2 Mentor, our mission is to help student athletes develop, build confidence and challenge their talents and abilities; encouraging them to thrive in sports and education.

We take the under achieved student athlete and focus on building their confidence by putting them in the forefront of their peers; while keeping the excelling student athlete humble and on the right path.

During family visits, we assist with identifying the root that causes friction or disruption in the classroom or on the field.

Our goal is to assist students achieve their true potential. Whether in an athletic environment or educational setting, the team at Coach 2 Mentor ensures that the individual thrives and increases their level of self-confidence.

To request Coach Archie to speak at your next event, workshop, school, church or your organization, please call (240) 442-C2M8 or C2MPress@ArchieBeslow.com.

Please visit our website and join our mailing list so we can keep you informed of future events.

www.ArchieBeslow.com

To Contact the Author

Coach Archie Beslow
202-420-8486
coach@ArchieBeslow.com
www.ArchieBeslow.com

Please include your testimony or help received
from this book when you write.

Your prayer requests are also welcomed.

For Press & Media, please contact
C2MPress@ArchieBeslow.com
(240) 442-C2M8

TO ORDER MORE BOOKS:
www.ArchieBeslow.com
www.anointedpresspublishers.com
www.amazon.com
KINDLE

Ingram Distribution